Carpet Magic

First published in association with the
Barbican Art Gallery
as a companion to the exhibition
Carpet Magic 25 April to 19 June 1983

ISBN 0 946372 0 12

© Jon Thompson 1983
Designed by Trilokesh Mukherjee

Printed by Balding + Mansell Limited,
Wisbech, Cambridgeshire

A shepherd couple, Chamba valley, India.

Previous page: A man from Afghanistan

Carpet Magic

Jon Thompson

The art of carpets from the tents, cottages and workshops of Asia

Introduction

A new way of thinking about carpets

In the last ten years there has been a growing interest in carpets. Many books have appeared in this time, including catalogues, introductory texts and more specialised works covering new ground. Yet in spite of all the effort put into these publications the subject of carpets still bewilders and confuses most people. What seems to be needed is a basic framework of ideas that can be used in approaching this huge and perplexing field. The scheme set out here aims to provide this framework. Normally carpets are classified according to their country of origin, but the types produced within any one country are so dissimilar that grouping them together merely causes confusion. As a result many people are discouraged from following the subject any further. Here the geographical classification is abandoned and instead carpets are arranged in four groups according to the circumstances in which they were made. This is a new way of looking at carpets, and their division into four main categories is the underlying and unifying theme of this book. The four categories are: tribal weavings; products of the cottage industries; carpets manufactured in town or city workshops; and court carpets.

The cottage industry is made up of women working at home to increase their family income. Because they are weaving to sell, cottage weavers are less conservative than tribal weavers, are always on the look-out for new ideas, and are sensitive to what is in fashion. In common with tribal weavers they enjoy bold primary colours and use unsophisticated equipment. This prayer rug from Mujur, central Turkey, follows the once fashionable Ottoman court style but is interpreted with a typically rustic vigour and boldness. Nineteenth century.
183 × 130 cm.
Private collection.

The tribal weaver cannot retain in her memory the large complex patterns found in workshop carpets. Expressive power is achieved through the use of colour, space and proportion. This outstanding example of Turkmen tribal work illustrates the use of small, easily remembered patterns set in a perfectly balanced arrangement on a deep red ground. It was woven by a member of the Salor tribe of Turkestan before 1850. 47 × 111 cm.
Fritz Langauer of Adil Besim OHG, Vienna.

The four groups are arranged in order of increasing technical achievement. Our interest is centred on the carpets of the first three groups made between the seventeenth century and the present. Most were made in the nineteenth and early twentieth centuries. The fourth group, which is not covered in detail in this work, consists mainly of carpets made for the Islamic courts in the sixteenth and seventeenth centuries. They probably account for less than a tenth of one per cent of all surviving carpets made before 1900 and are mentioned for the sake of completeness and because they had an enormous influence on the design of later carpets belonging to the three other groups.

Those with expert knowledge will be quick to point out that the proposed divisions are not exact, so let me do it first by saying that to be concerned with exactness or lack of it is to miss the point. The classification is intended to provide a way of looking at carpets, an intellectual framework to be used as an aid in learning about them. As soon as a person acquires sufficient information of his own and has built up a store of his own observations then he can abandon the classification and devise one for himself. Part of the value of having such a scheme is that it obliges the user to search carefully for clues that will tell him what sort of carpet he is looking at. It is the effort made in trying to decide which category a carpet belongs to that is important and not how well it fits it. A lot can be learned in the process and things may be discovered which would otherwise have passed unnoticed. As a help towards this end the approach throughout this work is deliberately general, technical discussion is limited, jargon avoided, and no attempt is made to cover new ground in terms of attribution or to provide detailed information on classification. The aim is to take a bird's eye view of the whole field of carpets with the non-specialised reader in mind and examples of the different categories have been selected to give an idea of the great range of taste encompassed within the field.

One effect of the lack of a satisfactory working classification of carpets is that many museums with collections of carpets do not know what to do with them. The fact that they originate in an Islamic country is often sufficient to ensure that they end up in the department of Islamic art, where the great majority, since they have little to do with Islamic art, are treated as unwelcome clutter and put into storage. They might be in better company in a museum of anthropology, but I know of no major primitive or ethnographic art collection that has taken more than a passing interest in tribal carpets. The usual reason given is that there is no point in gathering a mass of unclassified material because objects, to have any value, must be collected directly from the producers and documented at the time. But since the tribal way of life is fast disappearing I believe it is shortsighted not to acquire carpets for collections on these grounds. After all, lack of knowledge concerning the source has not prevented European museums from building up spectacular collections of pre-Columbian textiles, pottery, metalwork and so on which as archaeological artefacts are completely unsatisfactory since their source is often unknown. It could take just one curator of a primitive art collection with an interest in the field to change the outlook of others and start a phase of serious scholarship in tribal carpets.

It was mentioned that the four categories are arranged in order of increasing technical development. Perhaps the main value of the classification is that it also describes four different artistic categories, though it must be emphasised that no judgement on the merit of each is implied. A progression in the artistic sense is present but only in that it mirrors the increasing technical elaboration. In the art of carpet weaving the progression is from those executed entirely from memory to those resulting from exact written-down instructions. I believe that the greatest source of confusion in carpets is a lack of understanding of the artistic differences between them which the classification should help to make clearer. Put very simply tribal carpets can be thought of as 'primitive art' (in the best sense of the word), and workshop carpets as 'decorative art'. As each has its own aesthetic logic, comparisons between carpets in different categories is meaningless.

To introduce such ideas is to tread on dangerous ground so perhaps I should explain a little more and at the same time define the categories in more detail.

Tribal carpets are not designed as such but woven directly from memory. They are primarily made for use, not sale, and, in addition to their practical role as grain sacks or pannier bags, have an important place in tribal life. They were and are used for when guests come, for weddings, as gifts, for picnics, prayer, the decoration of animals, the tent, the home and for every important aspect of life. Traditional and sacred patterns are woven into the rugs making them part of the very fabric of tribal life and identity, and the borders protect and enclose a space decorated with devices for the promotion of good fortune, fertility and for warding off evil influences. Some designs are used only by a particular tribe or on a special kind of object. All these patterns, charged with significance, can only be understood by reference to the culture of those that use them. Regrettably much tribal weaving found in the market place is little more than ethnographic junk, equivalent to the grass skirts and assagais of the ethnographic art market, and much that passes for tribal weaving has been made by weavers no longer constrained by the traditions and demands of tribal life. Among the tribal weavings of the nineteenth century are objects of surpassing beauty and a few have been selected to represent the best of tribal work in this book. Leaving aside the aspect of decay in tribal life, which is not peculiar to the carpet weaving communities, the best tribal carpets bear comparison with the best examples of the art of Africa, Oceania and the north-west coast of America, which are now widely acknowledged as art of a high order. Curiously the art of the north-west Pacific coast, based on certain design principles which were forgotten during the last century and recently 'rediscovered' by Holm,[1] has many parallels

Weaving began in Qom in the 1930s. It soon acquired a high reputation for quality of workmanship and originality of design. In Qom a sort of decentralised workshop system operates in which weavers work at home to standards normally found only in workshops. This rug has a design inspired by seventeenth-century Indian court carpets. It has highlights in silk and is typical of the high-quality work associated with Qom.
215 × 137 cm.
Apadana Carpets, Firouzan and Nematollahi.

The well-dressed horse wears a cover with two flaps which fasten at the front. They are usually flatwoven, but this twentieth-century example woven by a Turkmen tribe living in northern Persia, the Yomut, is worked in knotted pile.
109 × 102 cm.
L. Kelaty Ltd.

A typical item made for domestic use is the salt bag. This delicately patterned tribal weaving is the work of Baluchis in eastern Persia. It is not very old but shows no sign of the decline in standards so common in later tribal work. 56 × 38 cm. **Private collection.**

BELOW: Neighbouring Turkmen tribes have many designs in common yet weave in a technique and colour style unique to themselves. This bridal camel trapping of the Saryk tribe makes an interesting comparison with a similar object made by the Salor tribe (illus. p.30). 45 × 129 cm. **Private collection.**

LEFT: *In the Caucasus during the second half of the nineteenth century cottage weavers became extraordinarily inventive and created a whole new repertoire of rug designs. This Kazak carpet from the Karabagh district of the south Caucasus uses a design borrowed from a tie-dyed textile and combines it with a tree, stylised animals and little human figures in a highly individual composition. The two hands convey the idea of protection. Nineteenth century. 240 × 183 cm.*
Eskenazi, Milan.

RIGHT: *The severely abstract design of this carpet makes an interesting comparison with the work of some modern painters. It is made on a narrow loom in strips which are then sewn together. It has a shaggy, pelt-like quality unlike any other nomadic carpet and could be what the earliest piled carpets looked like. It is also unusual in that the strips are woven with natural undyed wool and then dyed in one piece. The source of such pieces is not known for certain. They appeared recently in Afghanistan and are said to be the work of Uzbegs. Some carpets of this type are shaped like the felt carpets of the Kirghiz (illus. p.77), in a broad curve as if to fit a tent, so they were probably made by tent dwellers. It is not even certain if there are any nomadic Uzbegs in Afghanistan. It may have come from some little-known nomadic group which has been caught up in recent political disturbances in the area. Possibly Afghanistan. After 1950. 305 × 107 cm.*
Private collection.

with the art of one of the most outstanding groups of tribal weavers, the Turkmen (Turkoman) of central Asia. I believe that the design-power, primal abstraction and profound character of some tribal and cottage-made weavings, a tradition maintained exclusively by women, will come as a surprise to many people who have never seen this type of work before. Likewise I shall be interested to learn what impression they make on people who have never considered carpets as art, and particularly lovers of twentieth-century abstract painting who should find much to excite them.

The art of the weaver working at home in her spare time, the backbone of the cottage industry, has at best some of the primordial quality of tribal weaving. But, unfettered by the traditions of tribal life and with a customer to satisfy, she can modify her work to suit the buyer. The character of the cottage-made carpet is moulded on the one hand by the weaver's preference for bright strong colours, and on the other by her desire to make something up-to-date, fashionable and saleable, which is expressed in a readiness to copy town carpets or even to devise entirely new patterns. In the Caucasus during the second half of the nineteenth century cottage weavers became extraordinarily inventive and created a whole new repertoire of rug designs using elements of traditional patterns and reworking them in an original way. These are now much in demand with collectors. Most cottage rugs are woven from memory or with the aid of a drawing. Sometimes a cartoon is used but not with the same exactitude as is demanded in the commercial workshops. They are distinguished from the tribal carpets by their more cosmopolitan designs and adaptability to the demands of the market. In character they occupy a middle place somewhere between tribal and workshop carpets.

The town and city workshops make carpets for

This small rug from the Shirvan district in the south Caucasus, a product of the cottage industry, shows great originality in its pure abstract design and use of colour. Those interested in contemporary painting may be surprised to learn that it was made in the nineteenth century. 122 × 91 cm.
Thornborough Galleries.

RIGHT: Silk dyed in brilliant colours gives force to the powerful abstract design of this striking rug, a product of the cottage industry in the Heriz district of north-west Persia. Nineteenth century. 144 × 92 cm.
Private collection.

The art of the workshop carpet is the art of the designer. This modern silk rug from the Hereke workshop, the source of Turkey's most refined carpets, has a pattern based on an eighteenth-century Indian design. 145 × 99 cm.
Cyrus Carpets.

Tents in the Engizek mountains. Atmali village, Marash province, Turkey.

A. U. Pope, one of the greatest scholars in the field of Persian art, wrote in 1926 'The elements of the design are like notes in a melody or words in a poem.' Rhythmical repetition, inversion and the varying combination of patterns give carpets a quality akin to that of music. This beautifully made rug from the nomadic Qashqai tribe of southern Persia uses a floral cluster pattern, or boteh *in a simple alternating rhythm, where the use of different colours create a secondary diagonal design. Nineteenth century.* 237 × 137 cm.
Nick Oundjian.

commerce by a production process. Instead of one person doing everything, production is split up into a number of specialised crafts. A designer makes an exact drawing in the form of a cartoon and the weavers follow it exactly, reproducing knot for knot the specified pattern. For them there is no question of any particular attachment to the carpet other than as a means of earning a living. Workshop carpets are thus designed in the same way as wallpaper or curtain fabric and in the modern home have a similar function. It is in this sense that the term 'decorative art' was used. After a long period of disfavour that began with Ruskin and lasted until recently, 'decorative art' has been reinstated and is now the subject of renewed interest. The tendency to deny it the status of genuine art is no longer tenable. Furthermore the twentieth-century exploration of all aspects of abstract art has, by way of reaction, brought back into focus problems of special interest to the designer, such as the use of pattern to order the space on a plane surface. With hostility to 'mere decoration' a thing of the past, ornament no longer a dirty word, and the designer acknowledged as an artist in his own right, designed carpets should be assured of a fair assessment. They will, I hope, be judged as art objects by the quality of their design and not compared to carpets of fundamentally dissimilar character such as those woven from memory.

Carpets and music

In trying to think and talk about carpets I find myself constantly comparing them with music. The warp and weft of their underlying structure are, like the musical stave, the vehicle for the pattern and impose upon it a basic order. Their visible surface is covered with thousands, sometimes millions, of tufts of wool and the resulting minute points of colour are arranged like the individual notes of a melody into motifs and patterns. There is a musical quality in the combination, inversion, repetition and rhythm of their patterns, and in their colour harmony and texture. Like music, the art of carpets is poorly supplied with terms capable of conveying the flavour of the experience they evoke. The achievement of an aesthetic effect by using space, colour, proportion and pattern gives some carpets a completely abstract quality which I find only in music. Musical comparisons are a recurring theme throughout this review so it may help to think of the four main streams of carpet production and design in terms of a musical analogy.

Carpets made by the nomads and tribeswomen have the character of folk music. The pattern, like a folk song, is learned by girls from their mothers as soon as they are old enough to help. It is not written down anywhere and is kept alive by direct transmission from person to person. A number of tunes or patterns known within a community resemble in a general way those of neighbouring communities while retaining a distinct and individual character. The communal repertoire is never static, new things are being absorbed and others forgotten all the time, but at a slow rate.

The cottage-made carpet is like the performance of a solo entertainer with a repertoire of popular and traditional songs.

In contrast the workshop carpet, especially the court carpet, resembles a concerto such as those Bach composed

LEFT: *As well as making carpets for sale, cottage weavers made items for domestic use, among them pileless rugs, using a weft wrapping (Soumak) technique. Like other domestic weavings their patterns, transmitted within communities from one generation to the next, tend to be conservative and as a result preserve designs in vogue centuries ago. This example has a design that appears in a carpet painted by Carlo Crivelli in the late fifteenth century. Nineteenth century. 321 × 185 cm.*

BELOW LEFT: *Weavings made and used by the nomadic (Yuruk) Karakoyun tribe. Summer pasture in the Taurus mountains, Nigde province, Turkey.*

BELOW: *One member of a Turkish nomad, or Yuruk, family on migration. The child is well strapped in and held in place by a large, elaborately decorated storage bag. Sarikechili tribe, Marash province.*

This recently made silk carpet from China is an interpretation of an Indian design of the eighteenth century produced for the Mughal court. The hand of the Chinese designer shows through where the strongly alternating line of the border, almost part of the traditional language of carpets, is interpreted with the eyes of someone accustomed to seeing plum blossom and coral. China. 244 × 168 cm.
L. Kelaty Ltd.

for the Duke of Brandenburg or Haydn for the court of Esterhazy. The concerto has a style, character and musical form created by the composer. Every note is exactly scored and the musicians give expression to the composition by playing precisely what is written down. Similarly the court carpet is 'composed' by a designer in a style compatible with his training, current fashion and the expectations of the patron. Every knot is specified in the pattern and the weavers, using all the skills acquired in a long training, convert signs on a piece of paper, knot by knot, into a carpet.

The history of carpet design has parallels in the history of music. Traditional dance forms, rhythms and melodies were a starting point for the elaborations of much European court music during the seventeenth and eighteenth centuries. Likewise the corpus of ideas and patterns constituting the tribal or folk tradition has acted as a sort of prime substance for the periodic development of the court carpets. Many of the basic ideas and forms of court carpets derive from earlier traditional forms. The movement of ideas in the opposite direction is more obvious. Designs emanating from the court workshops had a powerful and sustained influence on the patterns woven in the cottage industries and were even taken up by the less isolated tribes. They have also been the biggest single influence on the design of commercial carpets and remain so even today. Visual patterns, like ideas and musical melodies, have no real frontiers. They spread far beyond their point of origin and are kept alive by a vital series of communications, so difficult to follow that the pathway from person to person or place to place may never be known. There is a constant two-way flow towards and away from the two 'poles' of influence, the court circle and the rustic community.

The question of taste
Before dealing with each of the four weaving categories in more detail, some attempt must be made to address the problems of taste and aesthetic preference. Part of the reason for dividing carpets into the four streams is that they mirror the great divisions of taste. It was an education for me to witness the amazement and disbelief of an educated and successful Persian dealer, a recent refugee from Iran, when he saw the price paid at auction for a Kazak, a coarsely woven, crude looking Caucasian village carpet with a bold pattern and strong colours. 'They are so coarse and ugly,' he said. 'How can they pay so much money?' He was genuinely distressed. For him the ideal of beauty and desirability was a rug with a perfectly ordered, detailed pattern, finely and exquisitely worked in evenly balanced colours without any mistakes.

In contrast for many lovers of tribal and village rugs the typical Persian city-style carpet, with its fussy scrolls and plethora of minute ornaments covering the whole field, has no appeal. Their preference is for powerful designs, empty space and primary colours – 'The rug has gotta have guts,' as one American collector put it. The coarseness or fineness of weave is for them irrelevant, and inaccuracies or mistakes in the weaving, unless they are so gross as to be disfiguring, are regarded as pleasing irregularities – a feature of the hand-woven item. This idea of 'pleasing irregularities' is a target for intellectual jokes among anthropologists and for cynical amusement among others who feel that tolerance of 'irregularities' in

One reason for dividing carpets into four streams is that they mirror the great divisions of taste. At one extreme people prefer powerful designs, empty space and primary colours. Coarseness of weave is irrelevant and mistakes or inaccuracies, unless they are so gross as to be disfiguring, are regarded as pleasing irregularities. This Kazak rug, the product of a cottage industry in a south Caucasian village is in the typical 'primitive' style of many tribal and village carpets. Nineteenth century. 141 × 125 cm.
Private collection.

At the other extreme of taste is the preference for a perfectly ordered, detailed pattern, finely and exquisitely worked in evenly balanced colours without any mistakes. This recently made Esfahan carpet continues the long-established tradition in Persia of high-quality, workshop-made carpets. Knotted into the plain woven band at the lower end are the words 'Sarraf Mamoury'. 1970s. 240 × 148 cm.
Cyrus Carpets.

an object is the same as the inability to see its faults. This of course may be true but let someone with this view be fitted with a set of dentures of perfect regularity and he will not smile so readily. If uniformity and standardisation are so desirable, why is it that manufacturers of mass-produced, factory-made goods in the west like to give the impression that their products are actually home made? Is it the quality of wholesome freshness, the unspoiled honesty of the ingredients and the individual care in making something intended for personal use that appeals so much to us? For the lover of the 'home made' carpet, however, the perfectly made, regularised, commercial carpet has as much individuality as wallpaper. But in case the comparison to wallpaper appears pejorative, and before I wander too far from my theme, I must stress again that the division of carpets into categories carries no suggestion of one being better than the other. Let me illustrate the absurdity of comparing the divisions with one another by yet another example – when the claim is made that a coarse peasant rug from Loristan is 'better' or 'worse' than an elegantly designed and finely worked rug from Qom.

Let us consider first the Loristan rug made by a young bride to celebrate her wedding. Woven into the design are her name and that of her future husband, the date, and a variety of special charms, amulets and protective designs which she learned from her grandmother. It is to be used in her future home and will always have a special place in her affections. Somehow or other the rug passes out of the family and into a western household. Even in its new situation the rug conveys something of the feelings of the young weaver so many years ago. The colours are bright, strong and unsophisticated. The patterns have a naivety of execution which gives the rug an enduring freshness.

In contrast the Qom rug has a pattern drawn by an experienced designer, a popular one based on a classical prototype first used in Persia during the sixteenth century. The carpet was woven by a skilled weaver with fifteen years' experience, using the best woollen yarn for the pile. The final clipping and finishing was also carried out by a highly skilled craftsman. The end product seems to recapture something of the elegance of court life in former times, a perfect addition to the furnishings of a wealthy home.

So which is better? Arguments about the merits and shortcomings of art objects are pointless when the things being compared have so little in common. If you look for quality and refinement the Loristan rug is a crude whimsical contraption altogether lacking in merit. If the appeal lies in a sense of the weaver's presence, the charm, directness and childlike lack of sophistication with all the little mistakes and irregularities, then the Qom rug is contrived, mechanical, sterile and over-refined.

If there are some people with fixed ideas about what they like, there seem to be many more 'floating voters' influenced by what other people think and say. Fashions of taste exist in the field of carpets as much as any other and are a fascinating side of the art world. It is astonishing how the rare and valuable objects, collected at such expense in the face of fierce competition by our fathers and grandfathers, can be ignored by the fashionable mainstream of today. Succeeding generations overturn

Weavers in the Heriz district of north-west Persia, the centre of a large cottage industry, are noted for their ability to weave complex designs from a drawing without the use of a cartoon. This example, with its design of a mythological tree, was probably worked from an illustration in a book. Their silk carpets have an unusual and pleasing colour tonality with red-brown, light blue and a silvery ivory, which, together with the rustic interpretation of the complex curvilinear design, give them a character unlike any other Persian carpet. Nineteenth century. 235 × 185cm.
Nathan and Joseph Azizolahoff.

The first Indian carpets were designed by Persian artists, and only later took on a uniquely Indian character. The early connections between the two artistic cultures has given Persians a sympathy for Indian design, visible in this silk prayer rug from Kashan. It is based on an eighteenth-century Mughal original which it resembles in its exquisite workmanship and minute attention to detail. Designs originating in the court ateliers, often the work of the leading artists of the day, have been an unfailing source of inspiration to designers ever since. Nineteenth century. 216 × 137 cm.
Khalili Gallery.

BELOW: *Interesting and collectable tribal carpets are still being made today. This little prayer rug, worked mainly in plainweave and partly in knotted pile has a delightful simplicity in the imagination of its design. Pul-i-Kumri village, north-east Afghanistan. 1970s.* 125 × 76 cm.
The Rug Shop.

received opinions; old ideas are dropped and replaced by new criteria of judgement. Sixty years ago the carpets most popular in Europe were cottage-made Turkish rugs of the eighteenth and early nineteenth century. In the eighteenth century there was a vogue in Turkish high society for French architecture and decoration, and true to form rugs made in the cottage industry at the time incorporated features of the new fashionable style. Their refinement, soft colours and tendency towards elaboration had a sympathy with the Louis XV gilt and ormolu style favoured since the eighteenth century by the wealthy of Europe, so they fitted well with prevailing ideas of good taste in the west. Today, in keeping with the spirit of our times, there is an adventurousness in taste, a willingness to accept the unfamiliar and to enjoy the abstract. The derivative is rejected in favour of the primal, the elemental is preferred to the elaborate, the austere to the cosy. The rugs in fashion sixty years ago are no longer thought of, and in real terms have fallen to between a half and a tenth of their value in the 1920s.

The time is ripe, I believe, for a renewed public interest in carpets. For those experienced in other fields of art, such as painting, the division of carpets into four categories should provide a short cut to their aesthetic appreciation. For those who have never seen carpets as anything other than floor covering I hope it will be the beginning of a new awareness. If my hope is realised and this view of carpets brings people to the point of wishing to buy carpets because they love them, it is as well to point out that court carpets are too rare to be worth collecting without considerable knowledge and means. There are however plenty of possibilities in cottage rugs, and interesting inexpensive tribal rugs are still being made today (illus. p.29). There is even an elite band of collectors, often people who have lived in Persia and acquired a taste for the subtleties of Persian design, who buy and keep only the finest and most outstanding workshop carpets.

I have often wondered if it is possible to look at the taste and opinions of today with the eyes of a historian living a hundred years in the future. Can those works of art destined to be acknowledged as masterpieces in time to come be recognised today? I do not claim that all or even half the examples of the categories shown here are masterpieces of the art of carpets. They have been selected to give an idea of the great range of taste encompassed in the field of carpets. But there are enough outstanding examples for the person with artistic awareness but no previous experience to have the pleasure and excitement of seeing if he can discover them for himself.

The source of this kilim is unknown, but its interest lies in the border details. It must have been made to celebrate a wedding because the couple are shown together with hookah, fish, animals, samovars and teapots – expressing the hope for enjoyment and plenty in the future. The date is hard to read – it may be 1294 which corresponds to AD 1877. Possibly Azerbaijan. 458 × 200 cm.
Bolours of London.

Some of the most appealing modern tribal weavings are those made by nomadic people in the Fars district of south Persia and known as Gabeh rugs, a local nickname for coarse pieces of uncertain origin. They display in their designs an unclouded vision and directness of expression like that of children. They have as a result an exhilarating freshness and vitality. They are inexpensive and deserve greater recognition. Mid twentieth century. 183 × 100 cm.
London Oriental Carpets Ltd.

RIGHT: *This carpet is a rare survival of a vanished tradition. It was used to cover the entrance to a Turkmen tent and a magnificent spectacle it must have been. It is some time since piled rugs have been used for this purpose and, although their use is remembered by the Turkmen, no photograph of a piled door rug in use has ever been published. Furthermore the tribal group which made this piece was virtually extinguished in the mid-nineteenth century. It is one of three known surviving examples of Salor workmanship. Tribal carpets are often consigned to deep storage in the Islamic department of the few museums which have them, whereas it would be more appropriate for them to be looked after by ethnographers. Efforts to acquire material of this quality should be made by museums of ethnography. Nineteenth century.* 182 × 129 cm.
Private collection.

A Kirghiz woman.

BELOW: *This trapping, with its deep colours and large, rounded, well balanced designs, has an air of calm gravity. It is extraordinary to think that this is an example of the art of young Turkmen women. In Turkmen culture woven objects are part of the very fabric of tribal life and skill in weaving is a valuable and respected asset. Salor tribe, nineteenth century.* 75 × 170 cm.
Private collection.

Chapter one

Western interest in the eastern carpet

Early interest

You may be treading on a work of art without knowing it. If you think this is an over-dramatic statement you should know that remarkable treasures are being sold from homes and estates all the time, and that the owners seldom have any idea of their importance before the sale. So if you have a rug at home bought more than fifty years ago there is a chance that it could be something exciting. It is not only the public who have difficulty in understanding carpets. Of all the objects circulating on the art market carpets are probably the least understood, so let us look at how these carpets came to the west and see how this state of affairs came about.

Carpets came to the west throughout the sixteenth and seventeenth centuries as objects of value which conferred dignity and status on their owners, as many paintings of the period reveal (illus. p.32). King Henry VIII had a sizeable collection of carpets and must have had an important influence on their popularity. Portraits showing him standing on recognisable Turkish carpets,

Carpets came to the west throughout the sixteenth and seventeenth centuries as rare and valuable items. Their popularity at the court of King Henry VIII encouraged the powerful and wealthy to use them as status symbols. Here Richard Sackville, third Earl of Dorset, is shown standing on a carpet. The artist has painted the carpet in sufficient detail for it to be identified as a type made in Turkey. Its source was probably a cottage industry which successfully supplied large numbers of carpets to Europe during the seventeenth century. William Larkin (fl.1610–1620). Richard Sackville third Earl of Dorset. Oil on canvas, 1613. 203 × 119 cm. **Suffolk Collection, Rangers House, Blackheath, London.**

BELOW: *A carpet of the type shown in Richard Sackville's portrait, the product of a seventeenth-century cottage industry in western Turkey which successfully supplied a flourishing export business to Europe. 207 × 150 cm.* **Keir collection.**

'*A Nubian model reclining*' *by Roger Fenton, a photograph taken in the late 1850s, which, in common with the orientalist painters, seeks to capture the flavour of the Middle East. She is lying on a rug from Megri, western Turkey.*

or seated on a carpet-covered podium, bear witness to their importance; so much so that copies of Turkish carpets were made in sixteenth-century England during the reign of Queen Elizabeth I. Turkey seems to have been the main supplier to the west through Venice and as a result all hand-knotted carpets, whether from Persia or Egypt, were called at the time 'Turkey carpets'. Some idea of the different types of carpet imported to the west can be gained from a study of contemporary European painting.

In the seventeenth century interest in carpets grew to include Persian, Egyptian and Indian products but already in the first decade of the century a new style of European carpet, destined to displace the oriental carpet from fashion, had made its appearance in France. Later, during the reign of Louis XIV, a workshop making carpets for the court was established in an old soap factory on the outskirts of Paris. The name '*Savonnerie*' became famous and the French decorative style was adopted as the norm of taste throughout Europe.

In the eighteenth century a designer commissioned to design an interior would include the floor covering in the overall scheme. It is known that the Adam brothers made their own carpet designs and had them executed in workshops in London and Axminster. Several other workshops are recorded as having been established in England and Scotland at this time to make hand-made pile carpets in European designs. The new décor made oriental carpets look unfashionable and demand for them faded away. It was at this time that the factories at Axminster and Wilton, now famous for machine-made carpets, began.

The rediscovery of carpets

In the nineteenth century 'oriental' or 'Persian' carpets as they came to be known again aroused interest. Paintings of nineteenth-century western interiors often include a rug or carpet, usually a tribal or village weaving from the Middle East (illus. p.36). Some of these were bought in the local bazaars and brought home by those tireless Victorian travellers, while others were imported by merchants from Turkey, which at the time was the centre of the carpet trade.

The resurgence of interest in carpets was stimulated by the so-called orientalist painters, artists working in the Middle East, who presented to the European public a romantic and dramatised view of local life. This type of painting, typified by the work of J. F. Lewis, became extremely popular. The subjects are meticulously drawn and frequently include representations of carpets that are on the whole accurate, just as they were in the sixteenth century, so that various types of piled carpet and flatweave can be identified without difficulty (illus. p.36). Research into European painting prior to 1700 has yielded important information on the dating of early carpets, and, in view of the difficulty of obtaining accurate data on the dating of tribal and village carpets, a similar approach could be used for later paintings. Nineteenth-century painting, potentially a rich source of information, has yet to be explored.

A few early photographs also include recognisable carpets, notably the work of Roger Fenton in the 1850s (illus. p.34). He, like the orientalist painters, attempted to capture something of the flavour of the Middle East.

One result of the increasing awareness of oriental carpets was the interest taken in them by William Morris.

Interest in carpets during the nineteenth century is mirrored in the work of William Morris who set up a commercial workshop in 1879 at Hammersmith. His designs were influenced by those of Persian carpets. Carpets made at Hammersmith by the River Thames between 1879 and 1881 are signed with his device consisting of an M, hammer and double wavy line signifying water.
William Morris, Hammersmith workshop, 1879–1881. 180 × 120 cm.
Joseph Lavian.

LEFT: *Nineteenth-century paintings often include identifiable carpets and are potentially a rich source of information on the dating of tribal and village products. In this painting the carpet on the floor is a Turkmen tribal weaving, made probably by the Ersari tribe in Turkestan.*
Kate Hayllar (fl.1883–1898). Sunflowers and Hollyhocks. Watercolour, 1889. 49 × 42 cm.
Corporation of London.

RIGHT: *A Turkmen tribal carpet made by the Ersari tribe in Turkestan. In the late nineteenth century many Turkmen tribespeople, including those who wove this type of design, fled to northern Afghanistan and settled in tribal villages, living in tents during the summer and in mud brick houses in the winter. Carpets such as this, made before the migration, have a wide range of colours and are the ancestors of innumerable later 'Afghan' carpets. Nineteenth century. 275 × 206 cm.*
A. S. Crosby.

BELOW: *Interest in carpets was stimulated by the so-called orientalist painters, artists working in the Middle East, who presented to the European public a romantic view of local life. Here the artist portrays a number of identifiable carpets, including three Caucasian, a Turkish flatwoven prayer rug and an Uzbeg embroidery hanging over the balcony. An amusing feature, also found in other orientalist paintings, is the heightening of sense of drama by drawing the human figures to a scale much smaller than they would be in life.*
Charles Robertson RWS (1844–1891). A Carpet Sale in Cairo. Watercolour. 76 × 135 cm.
Mathaf Gallery.

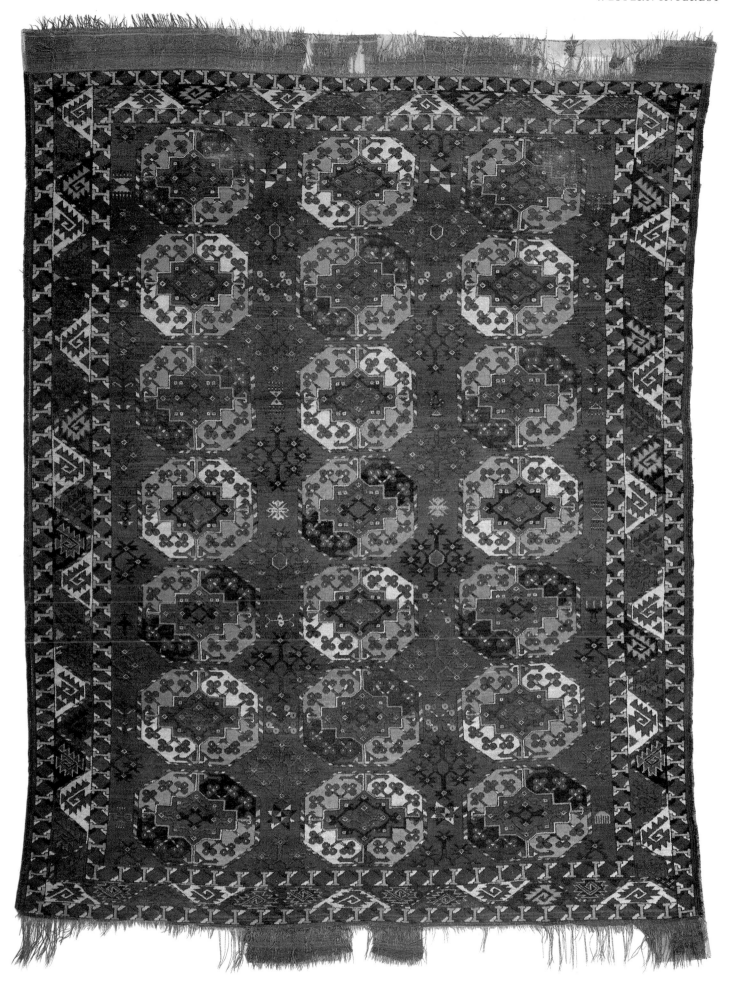

Goods arriving by camel train at the OCM warehouse at Smyrna (Izmir). After 1902.

RIGHT: *This is the type of rug that came to the west from a remote village a hundred or more years ago. It has a delightful 'primitive' quality and is probably the work of a Kurdish tribe in north-west Persia, but could possibly be a Lori weaving. Nineteenth century. 287 × 142 cm.*
A. Zadah, Persian Carpets.

BELOW: *So few tribal artefacts reached the west in complete condition that many people are unaware that these wide strips were shallow bags with an integral back. They were hung on the wall of the tent and used for personal belongings. This bag is missing its tassels and hanging straps. The remains of both are still visible. The colour, style and design are typical of Tekke work before the penetration of western influence. 46 × 126 cm.*
Private collection.

His indebtedness to eastern, especially Persian, design is well known, but he appears to have been particularly interested in carpets and set up a workshop for their commercial production in 1879 at Hammersmith. His designs, while original and distinctive, draw heavily on Persian carpets for their inspiration. Those made in his workshop between 1879 and 1881 are signed with his device consisting of an M, hammer and double wavy line, signifying water (illus. p.35).

In the second half of the century demand for these exotic imports increased enormously and the carpet, formerly a curio, became an accepted article of furniture in the respectable home. The response to this demand had far-reaching social and economic consequences for the carpet producing countries. The whole pattern of production gradually changed, as did the carpets themselves.

The growth in demand increased steadily and it became apparent to the more far-sighted merchants that tribal and cottage weavers would not be able to supply the requirements of the market for much longer, and that some additional source of supply was needed. In the 1870s the first of a new wave of carpet producing workshops was set up in Tabriz in north-west Persia. Others soon followed, and from these small beginnings grew Persia's huge commercial carpet manufacturing industry which has since been successfully copied in many other countries. We will look at this important development in more detail later. First we must look at how the carpet producing countries responded to increased demand prior to the great expansion of commercial production.

Exporters, hungry for goods, prompted enterprising local traders to visit the nomadic encampments, tribal areas and villages, and buy wherever the ancient craft was to be found, usually on a price per unit area basis. They then brought their wares to the trading centres such as Bukhara, Shiraz, Mashhad, Tabriz and Tiflis, from where they were transported in bales by camel, mostly to Constantinople, as it was called at the time, and then shipped to the west, having passed through several hands on the way.

As well as carpets and rugs the traders bought many items made for everyday use in tribal life, such as saddle bags, pouches and animal trappings. But what began as a basically functional object was not necessarily what

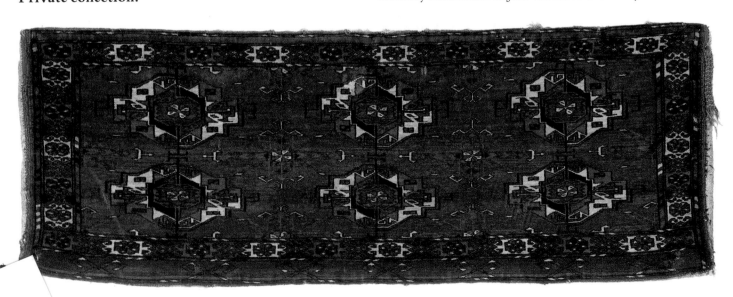

Mohair divan, no.801 from the brochure of Koch and te Kock, 1906. The use of tribal rug patterns for machine-made upholstery material was prompted by the vogue for cutting up tribal rugs for the purpose.

Carl Wilhelm Koch, born 1855, proud inventor of the tribal-style upholstery fabric.

BELOW: *In the 1870s and 1880s there was a fashion for cutting up tribal carpets and using them as upholstery material. This basically destructive practice has caused a few old tribal weavings to survive which might have been destroyed if used on the floor. Here bits of two carpets made by the Turkmen Tekke tribe have been used.*
Heskia, London.

ended up in the Victorian drawing room. The saleable part of these tribal weavings was the piled area and so appendages such as ropes, tassels, hanging loops and the plain-woven backs of bags were considered a nuisance, and their shipment an unnecessary cost. They were cut off, sometimes very crudely, and simply discarded. Objects were often further mutilated to make them more acceptable: cradle-shaped bedding bags were cut up into six pieces and sold separately as little mats to cover furniture; pairs of bags were sewn together to make a small rug after a border was cut from each; 40-feet long piled bands, used to stabilise the trellis tent, were cut into 3-feet lengths, and so on.

In the 1870s and 1880s many of these small tribal weavings were cut up and used as upholstery fabric, pillows and bolster covers. Ironically this basically destructive practice has caused a number of lovely old pieces to survive which otherwise might have been lost if used on the floor. An amusing aside to this fashion is that its popularity prompted the German firm of Koch and te Kock to produce machine-made imitations of Turkmen and Qashgai weavings for sale as upholstery material.

The objects reaching the west were faced with another menace, a process known as 'chemical washing', which involves treatment of carpets with alkali followed by an acid to neutralise the alkali. Sometimes a bleaching agent is used as well. This process partially degrades the wool, softening and increasing the lustre of the pile. The colours are also altered, toned down and even bleached out if desired. The aim is to make a more attractive product. The majority of new carpets sold today have been 'washed' under controlled conditions, but in former times the finer points were not always observed and many tribal artefacts, especially those bleached, have been completely ruined by the process. Objects surviving the twin hazards of mutilation and bleaching were then subjected to shod feet and the caresses of the older type of 'beat-as-they-bash-as-they-chew' vacuum cleaners. As a result few tribal weavings made prior to the impact of European influences survive in original or complete condition.

RIGHT: *Many carpets have come to the west without any documentary information about their source. This wonderful carpet, variously classified as Caucasian, Armenian, and north-west Persian, is such a piece. The technique is that of a Persian carpet, the colouring rustic, the design distantly derived from the prayer rugs of sixteenth-century Ottoman Turkey. It was probably made before 1800 and could well be a tribal version of a more sophisticated pattern. 270 × 155 cm.*
L. Kelaty Ltd.

LEFT: *Another carpet of uncertain origin is this piece from the south Caucasus. The field design is an adaptation of a textile pattern by an inventive cottage weaver, but the border is decorated with an old tribal motif usually used in the field. Nineteenth century.* 147 × 84 cm.
Richard Wright.

BELOW: *The inscription in this north-west Persian carpet has given rise to much discussion. The style and colouring is that of a piece made around 1900; the inscription refers to an order* made by Mizra Medhikhan in the time of Nader, dated 1124 or AD 1712. There are obviously two possibilities: that the date is wrong, or that our understanding of dating on the basis of colour and style is wrong. An inscription cannot always be relied on because it is a common practice in Persia for a craftsman to re-use the inscription present on some respected object in his own work, thereby conferring dignity upon it. If however the date is correct it will bring about some rethinking in carpet circles.* 335 × 238 cm.
Bolours of London.

A loaded camel of the Shahsavan tribe on Mount Savalan, north-west Persia, carrying two woven bedding bags.

Obscure sources, unsuspected treasures

Throughout this period no effort was made to keep records of the sources of the carpets. The traders who made first contact with the weavers certainly had every commercial reason to conceal their sources so it is very unlikely that in their turn the exporters in Constantinople had any more than a general idea of the district where the goods came from. Thus a mass of material of diverse ethnic and tribal origins, from villages and encampments all over Turkey, the Caucasus, Afghanistan and Persia, poured onto the market without any form of documentation, was shipped to Europe and America and sold to the public as home furnishings. And the further the carpets travelled from their origin the less people knew about them. It will ever be regretted that there were no ethnographers at this time making notes, recording dates, places and types of loom used; no Captain Cooks to bring to the west objects of known date and origin. Now there is only the carpets.

So how was the nineteenth-century householder to know what he was buying? The seller's knowledge was patchy, the buyer's ignorance total. The dealer would no doubt have done his best to tell the totally ignorant buyer all he knew about the pieces. In the case of tribal work little information of a specific nature was available but for commercially produced rugs there was more and it was generally accurate. Some valuable information has been transmitted by word of mouth within the families of dealers in the west, traditionally Armenians and Sephardic Jews, in the form of a lore of carpets, consisting of a sort of working jargon used in the everyday affairs of business. It includes an elaborate nomenclature, almost a set of nicknames, for carpets according to size, colour, pattern, place of shipment, district of origin, tribal origin, village of origin, function, shape and so on. Many terms are words from one of the local languages. As they have probably passed through at least one other language on their way to English the words have often changed into something else and their original meaning lost, giving endless opportunity for misunderstanding.[2] Much of the traditional information about carpets is valuable and amounts to the only source we have, but the accumulated inaccuracies will take a generation of scholarship to untangle. More than fifty years of study has already gone into laying the academic foundations for an understanding of the earlier Islamic carpets, but the classification and documentation of tribal carpets is still a long way behind.

The student of this material is faced with immense problems. In Europe the first tribal carpets came to museums as late as the 1870s. The haphazard gathering of tribal and village weavings has made it very difficult to understand the pattern of production at this time and as a result there are large gaps in the knowledge of where and when a piece was made. Occasionally the gap can be filled by the discovery of old inventories describing a particular carpet still in a house, or by an inscription and date woven into a carpet, but more often only an informed guess is possible. To complicate matters dates can be falsified and inscriptions are sometimes copied from earlier carpets. Perhaps somewhere there are documented examples of earlier date yet to be discovered, surviving under unusual circumstances, but although in the last ten years increased interest in tribal

RIGHT: *Some nomadic groups store and transport their bedding in special six-sided bags (above), which are often mistaken for cradles. This is the base and both long sides of such a bag. It is of exceptional quality and is probably the work of the Kashkuli, a division of the Qashqai tribe. Nineteenth century.* 180 × 131 cm.
London Oriental Carpets Ltd.

RIGHT: *Settled villagers of Bakhtiyari origin in the Char Mahal district of Persia were organised into a cottage industry at least as far back as the early nineteenth century. Their carpets are notable for their excellent wool and clear colours. They occasionally made carpets of large size. The inscription indicates that it was made on the order of the Ilkhan of the Bakhtiyari, a royal appointee, in 1323, which corresponds to AD 1905. The Bakhtiyari villagers must have continued to employ traditional technology well into the twentieth century, as no synthetic dyes have been used in this piece.* 186 × 132 cm.
Joseph Lavian.

BELOW: *The carpet has narrowly escaped destruction by passing feet, but the vitality and freshness of the multi-coloured flowers remains. In rural Kurdestan the craft of dyeing was maintained at a high level. Nineteenth century.* 274 × 168 cm.
Clive Rogers, Oriental Rugs.

Promoting the exotic. Mr Garabed T. Pushman, a native of Turkey, displays his handiwork, 'the first rug woven in Chicago', 1905.

RIGHT: *Nomadic Baluchis in Baluchistan, the arid regions of south-east Persia and south Pakistan, produce pileless weavings. Today the distinctive dark and handsome Baluchi piled carpets are the product of settled villagers in Khorasan, north-east Persia. There are indications that in former times the Baluchis of Khorasan had a more tribal life-style than they do today. They may therefore be latecomers to the cottage industry. This carpet is probably one of the oldest and by common consent one of the most beautiful examples known. It is reported that its previous owner was unaware of its quality. Nineteenth century. 240 × 162 cm.*
Wher collection.

weavings has brought to light numerous examples hidden away in museum storages and country houses, unfortunately none has had with it this much hoped-for paperwork.

This is how in the scramble to export goods during the last century a few objects, now understood to rank among the outstanding achievements of tribal and folk art, came to be used as scatter rugs, cushions, covers for piano stools, upholstery, and simply floor covering. Age is no guarantee of quality and in case the impression has been given that every old carpet is a masterpiece of ethnic art, it is good to remember that most carpets were the consumer goods of the tribal people, made for everyday use. They were discarded when worn and new ones woven to replace the old. Weavers with great skill and artistic sensibility were few, and only rarely did a weaving pass beyond the threshold of the ordinary. Such a variety and profusion of objects came onto the market in so short a time that it was impossible for traders and public to make detailed judgements on their character. Everything was mixed up and only now, with the benefit of hindsight, is it possible to discriminate between the exceptional and the commonplace.

If a buyer had a good eye he might pick out a particularly charming piece. But mostly purchases were on the basis of price, size and colour. Price was determined by size, fineness of weave and quality of workmanship, with a premium for rarity and special appeal. As a result of this haphazard process many a treasure has been pounded into oblivion by passing feet, although almost miraculously some outstanding objects have been lovingly cherished in quite modest homes to be passed on to the next generation.

A more common story is that the owner of an old carpet, unaware that the rug the dog likes to chew is a work of art is surprised at the interest generated by their old mat. The incomprehension of some owners is marvellous. A collector related to me how he found a fragment of an ancient Turkmen tent door rug, the oldest he had ever seen, in a dog basket. This was pointed out to the owner who not only refused to part with it under any circumstances but also declined to remove her dog's bedding from its normal place. She did, however, consent to allow it to be documented and photographed. A neighbour keeps a valuable and beautiful Caucasian rug in the hallway to prevent the wall-to-wall carpeting from being soiled by dirty feet and children's bicycles. The cost of carpeting the whole house twice over would not match the value of the rug.

In time the carpets bought long ago by grandparents or great aunts return to the market. The recycling of rugs from households back onto the market is a slow process. It may take as little as a decade or as much as three generations. Today we search among these old pieces innocently acquired so many years ago for treasures of a vanishing art which was already in decline a hundred years ago.

Chapter two

Making a carpet

Learning the craft

For as long as anyone can remember women in various parts of Asia have been weaving carpets at home. Girls learn to weave as soon as they are old enough to have the manual dexterity. Their first efforts are often made on a miniature toy loom. When they are skilled enough to make a real contribution they work alongside their mother or grandmother and other members of the family on the household carpet learning the patterns, and by the time they reach their teens they are proficient weavers, but this is only one phase in the making of a carpet. There are the other skills to be learned: wool sorting, combing, spinning, plying, stringing the warps onto the loom prior to weaving and cutting the pile of the finished carpet. Mastery of these skills means that a usable carpet can be produced without leaving the family and home. In this respect and in terms of basic skills tribal and cottage weavers are in the same position so the description of the carpet making process that follows applies equally to both. The main difference between them is in the type of loom used. Cottage weavers use an upright loom instead of the horizontal loom favoured by the nomads.

The materials

A carpet maker must know how to choose suitable wool for the various yarns used in a carpet. Basic wool quality is determined by the breed of sheep and not their diet or the climate, but in different parts of the same fleece there are quite large variations in quality. The best wool comes from a sheep's first clip and thereafter from the area around the neck and shoulders. When a sheep is sheared the fleece is pulled apart by hand and the clumps put into heaps of graded quality. The inferior wool is processed into felt and the better grades reserved for weaving. A different type of yarn is used for the warp, weft and pile, and the top quality wool is reserved for the pile. In making a selection an experienced wool sorter can distinguish differences in fibre diameter of three thousandths of a millimetre. Sorting wool by appearance and hand is still preferred to mechanical methods in the west.

The wool is then prepared for spinning by making it into loose, porous coils using a special wool comb (illus. p.54). The wool is pulled, using both hands, through long metal spikes set vertically in a triangular wooden frame, usually held between the knees. The purpose of this is to arrange the wool fibres so that they all lie parallel to each other. When spun, the resulting yarn is hard, smooth and lustrous, characteristics essential for the pile yarn. Alternatively the wool can be prepared for spinning by carding. Handfuls of wool are worked into a loose fluffy ball by pulling it repeatedly in different directions between two sets of teeth embedded in hand-held wooden carding implements (illus. p.54). The aim of

BELOW: *Drying freshly washed wool. Malatya province, Turkey.*

BELOW RIGHT: *Kirghiz women prepare wool for making felt by teasing it apart with a light wand, raising a cloud of dust in the process.*

carding is the exact opposite of combing, it is to randomise the fibres so that they all lie in different directions. Yarn spun from carded wool is soft, fuzzy, reflects little light and, compared to yarn spun from combed wool, has a greater strength for the same diameter. This kind of yarn is used for clothing and blankets where softness and insulation are important. As a rule combed wool is used for all carpets, kilims and flatwoven items.

The coils of prepared wool are then twisted into a thread by spinning. The basic spinning implement is the hand-held spindle. A strand is drawn out from the coil of combed wool and attached to the spindle which is rolled on the thigh or twisted between the thumb and fingers to set it in motion. The spindle is allowed to hang from the thread being formed and its rotation imparts twist to the thread which gradually lengthens as more wool is teased out of the coil. The loose coils of wool are kept under the arm, up the sleeve, wound lightly round the wrist or on a distaff. When the spindle reaches the ground it is taken up and in a neat motion the thread is wound onto the spindle and the process repeated. Women can be seen spinning with practised ease while watching the animals and children out in the fields or walking along the road. The hand-powered spinning wheel is also in common use (illus. p.54). Yarns for the weft are thin and loosely spun for flexibility, warp yarns are thicker and more tightly spun for strength, and the pile yarn is thick and loosely spun.

Warp and pile yarns invariably have two or more strands twisted together. Making a thicker yarn by

combining single threads is the process of plying and requires a special winding apparatus. Alternatively paired threads can be twisted (in the opposite direction to spinning) using a spindle (illus. p.55). After plying the yarns are wound into hanks for dyeing.

In former times women took their hanks of wool to the dyer; some still do but the single-stage new direct dyes are easier to use and much dyeing is now done at home. The results are not always happy. The dyed wool is wound into balls in readiness for weaving.

Weaving

Next the loom, which in essence is a rectangular frame, is prepared. The loom is set up in the protection of the main dwelling, inside or just outside. Warps are stretched between the two cross-beams and held under tension by the two sides of the frame. The preparation of the foundation is time-consuming, but must be meticulously accurate to avoid distortions when the carpet is finished.

Knots are 'tied' or wrapped round a pair of warps so that the two ends face the weaver. The two ends are cut with a hand-held knife leaving a double tuft sticking out. When a horizontal line of knots is complete a weft is passed across and back, over and under alternate warps. The wefts are packed or beaten down with a beating comb onto the row of knots to hold them in place. As weaving proceeds the pile is only roughly sheared with scissors since the final clipping is part of the finishing process. Thus the carpet is built up in alternating lines of knots and wefts. Tying knots is not difficult by itself. The main physical skills are getting the tension of the knots

Felt, a woollen cloth made without weaving, is an important material for nomads living in a harsh climate. It is used to cover the outside of the tent and on the floor inside. The felts of this tent are in poor shape and this Kirghiz family is making a new one. Felt is made by placing fluffed-up wool in an even layer, pouring soap and water on it and then compressing it repeatedly. Compression is being applied here by making the felt into a tight roll and rolling it backwards and forwards with the forearms.

RIGHT: *This woman is plying together two strands of yarn using a spindle. To do this she turns the spindle in the opposite direction to that used in spinning, setting it in motion by rolling it on her thigh. Plying is more commonly done with a winding device. Sinanli village in the Malatya province of central Turkey.*

LEFT: *The hand-powered spinning wheel is in use all over Asia. This Indian woman is using a well made model to spin carded wool for blanket making. The carding implements and the loose ball of carded wool are on the floor in front of her.*

BELOW: *Spinning wool with a spindle in Turkey. Loose porous coils of combed wool are wrapped round one wrist and, while the spindle is spinning round, an even strand is gently drawn out from the coil with the other hand.*

BELOW LEFT: *A Turkmen woman of the Yomut tribe combing wool by the traditional method.*

RIGHT: *Turkmen girls weaving a traditional tribal carpet on a horizontal loom. After making the knot they cut the tufts of the pile with a curved knife. Similar knives have been found in Russian Turkestan, together with spindles and needles, in women's graves dating from around 1400 BC.*

BELOW LEFT: *The felt hat identifies him as a member of the Qashqai tribe of southern Persia.*

BELOW: *A simple winder is used to make skeins from the spun wool prior to dyeing.*

A girl demonstrating the use of the beating comb, which is used to compact the line of knots after the insertion of the wefts. Tunisia.

and wefts even and compacting the knots evenly so as to get straight lines. The most impressive skill is a mental one, best appreciated by drawing a carpet pattern on paper, then trying to draw it from memory. The first will turn out to be difficult, the second out of the question. The exercise shows the precision required in converting a pattern from memory or from a cartoon into rows of coloured knots which, when viewed together, make up the pattern of the carpet. It is impossible to go back and correct mistakes, so weaving a successful pattern depends on the ability to plan the exact arrangements of the knots from the beginning. There are other little things to be learned, such as how to finish the sides and the ends. The sides are strengthened with extra wrapping material as each line of knots is added, and the warp ends tied or braided in a variety of ways to prevent the ends from unravelling. The women of the house weave together or separately whenever they have time between their various household duties. The activity can be surprisingly lively. The women may sing together and their work is punctuated by the rhythmical pounding of the beating combs and the tinkling of the little horseshoe-shaped pieces of metal that decorate them. Depending on the size several months' work may be needed to complete a carpet.

When it is finished the carpet is cut from the loom and the pile is sheared to its final length. In workshops a razor-sharp curved knife held in both hands is placed on the surface of the carpet and drawn towards the user, shaving the pile a little with each stroke. The more common method is to use scissors, sometimes with a projection at the tip of both blades so that extra pressure and control can be applied with the other hand. The best result is achieved by using fairly heavy pressure on the pile and shearing it by minute degrees dozens of times. This laborious work has the effect of polishing the wool and unravelling the twist in the pile wool so that the fibres in each tuft lie parallel. Both actions increase the lustre of the pile.

Before sale many carpets are washed with soap in a local stream or river, to remove accumulated dust. It is said that some streams are especially good for bringing out the colours. For instance the shade of red in wool dyed with madder can be altered by the acidity or alkalinity of the water and this may be the reason for the claim, but the softness of the water could also be a factor.

Colours and dyes

As we shall see, dyeing was in former times a family trade practised by the settled population. Although the methods used were often kept secret some of the processes are well known and others can be reconstructed by analysis of the dyes present in small samples of a yarn.

Blue is invariably produced with indigo obtained by a complicated process from plant material, and usually imported from India. The dye attaches directly to a woollen yarn. At first dip the colour is pale blue. With each successive dip the colour darkens a little. After repeated dyeing the blue becomes so dark it is almost black. Midnight blue, a colour particularly valued in the traditional Persian canon of taste is thus extremely expensive to produce (illus. p.61).

Red is obtained from madder which is extracted from the root of a widely available shrub. It does not attach

Washing carpets in a stream to remove dust prior to sale.
Dowlatabad, south Persia.

Many important carpets were woven in Khorasan, north-east Persia, in the sixteenth and seventeenth centuries. Production in the area has never ceased and in the nineteenth century, while other centres were in difficulty, carpets harking back to classical times were still being produced. This magnificent carpet has the deep-blue field so loved by Persians, produced by the expensive and laborious process of repeatedly dyeing a batch of wool with indigo. The scale of this carpet, its classical character and perfectly balanced field composition argue that this is a workshop product, but the border turns the corners unevenly so cannot have been worked from a detailed cartoon. It could well be the product of a cottage industry, perhaps in the village of Dorokhsh. Nineteenth century. 589 × 269 cm.
Heskia, London.

Indigo dyeing. Here cloth is being dyed after it has been woven. Depth of colour is achieved by repeated dipping. The broad expanse of midnight blue, so popular with Persians, is therefore expensive to obtain (illus. opposite).

directly to wool but requires a metal salt, normally of iron or aluminium to act as a mordant or link between the wool fibre and the dye. Madder is not one substance but a mixture of three major and three minor components. The amount of each varies with the age of the plant. By choosing madder plants of different age and using different combinations of alum and iron salts it is possible to obtain colours ranging from a brilliant scarlet (illus. p.31) through brown to deep purple (illus. p.73).

Yellow is obtained from a variety of plants but often the dye fades rather quickly on exposure to light. Green is obtained by dyeing wool in two separate operations with indigo and a yellow dye; likewise orange by adding a yellow to madder. Black is usually a combination of iron salts and tannin.

With indigo, madder, a yellow dye, black, natural brown and white wool the basic range of between six and thirteen colours can be obtained, the usual palette for tribal and cottage rugs. To these may be added a crimson dye obtained from an insect. The two commonest sources of it are lac from India and cochineal, originally from Mexico but since the nineteenth century cultivated in Europe.

Workshop carpets, and especially court carpets, commonly have a much larger palette, often over twenty shades and it is curious how the finest carpets of the four great Islamic courts all favoured the deep crimson red derived from lac and thought little of the scarlet red loved by the tribespeople.

ABOVE: *An important event in the life of any woman is her wedding. Among the Turkmen it was and is customary for young women to weave special hangings, often with a white ground, to decorate the bridal tent and the animals taking part in her wedding procession. This example was woven by the Salor tribe of Turkestan in the mid nineteenth century before synthetic dyes came into use. The brilliant effect is enlivened by the use of silk dyed with cochineal. Nineteenth century.*
48 × 140 cm.
David Black Oriental Carpets.

RIGHT: *A professional dyer from north Afghanistan.*

Effectively synthetic dyes began in the 1860s[3] but did not come into general use until the 1870s, reaching many of the nomadic tribes in the 1880s. Even so they were not adopted everywhere (illus. p.160). As is well known the early results were often disastrous: the colours were brilliant but they tended to fade or run, which gave them a bad name. Much interesting work has been done on synthetic dyes recently which has added greatly to the knowledge of carpets woven within the last hundred years. For example it is possible to tell sometimes where a rug is likely to have been made from a knowledge of the dye's source. A particular red dye used by the Turkmen has been identified as having been patented in Russia and pieces with this dye all appear to have been woven in Turkestan within the Russian sphere of influence, whereas in Afghanistan a synthetic yellow of British manufacture is found. Furthermore it is obvious that a rug dyed with a particular synthetic dye cannot have been made before that dye was marketed.

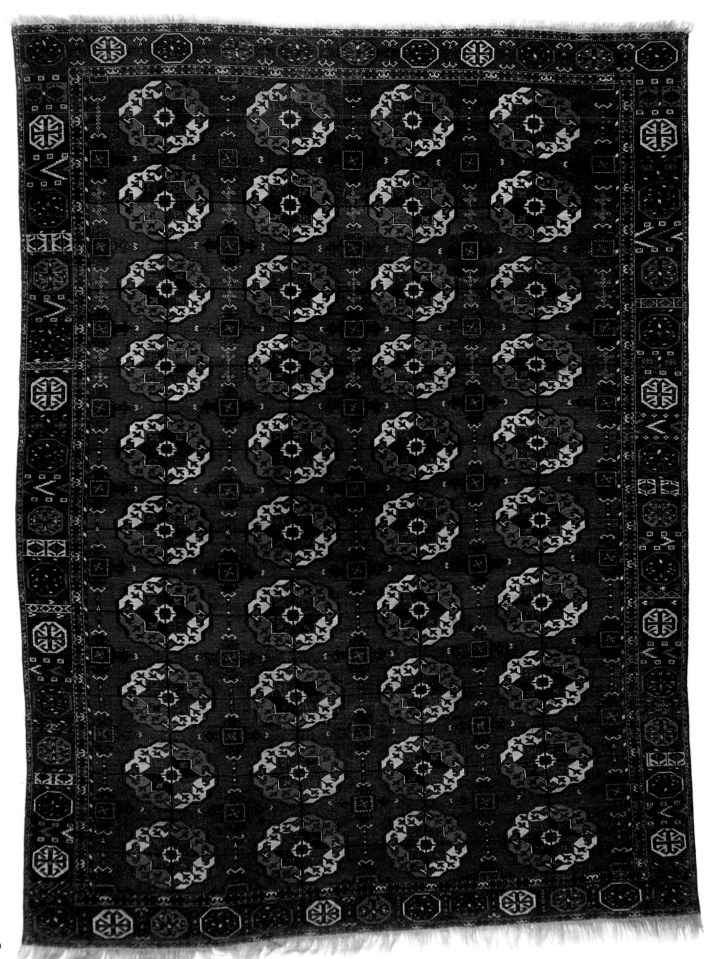

Chapter three

Tribal and domestic weavings

In the nineteenth century the Tekke were the dominant Turkmen tribe. Their carpets became famous in the west when, during the 1870s, the Tekke came under increasing military pressure from the Russian army, to be finally crushed in 1881. This was followed by a flood of Tekke carpets onto the market. These were shipped from the nearest commercial centre, which was Bukhara. They thus came to be known as Bukhara carpets, to which the title 'royal' was sometimes added to give them a spurious aura of importance. This carpet is an exceptional example of Tekke workmanship, both in quality and age, and its familiar gul *pattern has served as the inspiration for innumerable carpets from the workshops of Pakistan, and countless acres of machine made-carpets. Around 1800. 246 × 182 cm.*
Private collection.   Photo: Lefevre & Partners.

The origin and history of carpet weaving

I believe that the art and craft of the knotted pile carpet began where it has always flourished, among the pastoral nomads. Wool and leather are absolutely basic to their way of life. They are as much masters of wool as the ancient Egyptians were of stone. They process it into the covering for the roof and the walls of the tent, ropes, girths, bags and containers of all sorts, felt rugs for the floor, clothing for man and animals, and a variety of household items from oven gloves to blankets. It also serves them as a medium for artistic expression, for that deeply felt desire to make things pleasing to the eye, and the humblest item is decorated with a variety of colours and patterns. However only the more western tribes

Sunlight coming through the opening in the roof brings colour to the inside of the tent as Kirghiz women prepare food.

There is a custom in Turkey of giving a carpet to the local mosque. As a result Turkey has a richer inheritance of carpets and a more complete record of its carpet weaving history than any other country. The carpets covering the floor of this mosque in Karapinar are a good cross section of local production.

developed the knotted pile technique to a high technical and artistic level; the Mongols, who have a very similar life-style to the Kazakh, Kirghiz and Turkmen, have no knotted pile carpet tradition.

Many believe that the piled carpet had its origin in the desire to imitate something of the texture and insulating quality of animal pelts, a reasonable suggestion if we look at the shaggy Uzbeg carpet – a work of powerful simplicity (illus. p.11). Whatever the reason for the carpet's existence, many degrees of elaboration of it have existed since the earliest times. The frozen tomb at Pazyryk (mentioned later), which preserved in a great deep-freeze items of leather, wood, felt and silk, contained an almost complete finely knotted carpet 6 feet square and other fragments of coarser weave, now in the Hermitage Museum, Leningrad. These are the earliest surviving knotted pile weavings. Some believe that it was made by the nomads who buried it, while others say it came from urban Persia and was acquired as a gift or as booty in the same manner as the Chinese silks must have been. Technically it is not an object of particular virtuosity (in spite of claims to the contrary) compared to other contemporary crafts such as Chinese brocades.[4]

Apart from some poorly documented archaeological scraps from the sand-buried cities of east Turkestan (Sinkiang), and from the rubbish heaps of old Cairo, nothing more is known about the history of the carpet until the thirteenth or fourteenth century, the date of the earliest material from Turkish mosques. (As a result of the long-standing custom of giving carpets to the local mosque, Turkey has a richer inheritance of old carpets, and a more complete record of its carpet weaving history than any other country.) Practically every rug book calls a well-known group of early carpets found in a mosque in Konya Seljuk court carpets (i.e. twelfth or thirteenth century), but they have the character of cottage-made carpets and must have been made during the early Ottoman period some time after the year 1300.[5] However there are carpets in Turkey which could indeed be court products of the Seljuk period. They are of a much higher technical order than the Konya group, but they are little known and not yet on view to the public.[6] From the fifteenth century onwards there are enough surviving Turkish carpets to give a good idea of their history. In Persia there are practically no examples left prior to the seventeenth century. Many of the early examples have been preserved in the west but a fair number only left Persia within the last 125 years. These are mainly court carpets. The record of tribal and cottage-made carpets prior to the eighteenth century is very scanty.

Modern carpet history really began in the nineteenth century but to understand the pattern of production in each of the carpet producing countries it is necessary to know something of the history and composition of their peoples. Turkish carpets can be better understood if we remember that this formerly Greek-speaking country became, in the course of four and a half centuries beginning around AD 1000, increasingly dominated by the westward movement of Turkish-speaking people who were originally steppe nomads of Turkmen origin. Pockets of Greek speakers continued to live in western Turkey until the first quarter of this century when, as a result of war, there was a mass migration of them to

A striking effect is achieved by the use of blocks of colour on a white ground in this kilim, a good example of the earlier type of work from the Konya district of central Turkey. Nineteenth century. 395 × 163 cm.
Eskenazi, Milan.

Crete. Some may still remain in eastern Turkey. (The Greek community also wove carpets (illus. p.68 below), as the occasional inscription in Greek reveals, but the details of their output is unknown.) The nomad Turks migrated all over the country to find suitable pasture. Some settled down, but others have continued their nomadic life to the present day. Similar movements of people, in more than one wave, went into Persia, Azerbaijan, parts of the Caucasus, Turkestan, and parts of Afghanistan. In all these places there has been a trend towards settlement of these originally nomadic, Turkish-speaking people.

Wherever these nomads went there is a strong residue, more or less expressed, of Turkic design, but the longer the community has been settled the more diluted with other influences the designs have become. A typical example is the Ersari tribe, a large Turkmen group with many subdivisions, some of whom settled in the Oxus river valley during the seventeenth century. Their nineteenth-century weaving has a strongly tribal

RIGHT: *The colouring and decorative style of this carpet are immediately recognisable as the work of Turkmen weavers of the Ersari tribe settled in the Amu Darya (Oxus) river valley in the Emirate of Bukhara. But by no stretch of the imagination can this be thought of as tribal carpet. In fact the formerly nomadic Ersari had been settled since the seventeenth century and by the nineteenth century much of their output had taken on the character of a cottage industry. This huge carpet must have been made as a special commission for a palace or public building on a loom built for the purpose. Nineteenth century. 589 × 427 cm.*

Private collection.　　　　　Photo: Lefevre & Partners.

The two pannier bags, one being woven, the other hanging on the loom are the type of domestic weaving that rarely finds its way to the market place. Near Pannikale, Turkey.

character but, compared to their nomadic cousins' work, includes many assimilated elements from the patterns of Persian carpets and locally made silks. Carpet sizes are often more suitable for houses rather than tents (illus. p.71 opposite), and in many instances their work has taken on the character of a cottage industry.

Tribal communities

The term tribal is used here rather loosely as a practical description of carpets and the circumstances of their production and not as a definition of the social structure of a weaving community. It refers to weavings made primarily for personal use within a community. The tribal category includes the weavings of a few groups that arc unlikely to be accepted within the technical anthropological definition of the term. A better term might be tribal-style. The truly tribal groups, such as the Turkmen of Turkestan and the Qashgai of Iran, who are organised into clans or lineage groups and maintain some degree of large-scale tribal coherence, are typical producers of tribal-style carpets. But many weavings of similar character are also produced by peasant women in small village communities with no tribal allegiances, who are unaware of their larger relationships and often ignorant of their origins. These communities are often of particular interest because in their relative cultural isolation they may retain long-standing customs, an unusual life-style or even their own language. The term tribal is intended to exclude the products of communities where weaving is carried out solely as a means of livelihood, but does not exclude groups of weavings just because their makers sell a portion of them. Selling or bartering surplus weavings has always been a source of revenue for skilled tribal weavers.

Tribal and domestic weavings have a strong local, traditional, even cultic character and their traditional designs have often been in use with little change for many centuries. The point of excluding weavers working primarily for money is that market demand soon becomes an influence of such importance that it overrides any considerations of tribal convention or communal tradition. Weavers are then at the mercy of market pressures and soon they and their work are transformed into a cottage industry.

The output of such weavings is considerable and in addition to articles sold and exported there are innumerable domestic weavings made all over Asia which never reach the market place. There are communities in eastern and central Turkey, for example, whose weaving tradition might have gone unrecorded but for the discovery by ethnographers of old carpets in local mosques. Turkey in particular has a strong tradition of kilim, or pileless weaving, which has attracted serious attention only recently. Kilim weaving in Asia Minor or Turkey certainly antedates the arrival of the carpet weaving Turkic nomads in the eleventh century and appears to be an ancient and truly indigenous art form.

The numerous weaving communities, scattered in small, more or less independent groups throughout the carpet producing areas, have life-styles ranging from the pastoral nomadic to the settled agricultural. The most self-sufficient and independent of these live wholly in tents and move their flocks seasonally between summer and winter grazing. Others have both tents and houses,

BELOW: *In parts of Turkey piled carpets are used as a bed (Yatak). They are squarish and rather coarsely knotted. As they are purely domestic products their patterns tend to be conservative, which makes them difficult to date with any accuracy. This example has an archaic repeating pattern in many colour combinations with deliberate ambiguity between the motifs and the ground colour — both typical devices of the tribal weaver. Although probably made in the nineteenth century it could well be much earlier.* 198 × 167 cm.
Richard Lannowe Hall.

RIGHT: *Although the design of kilims tends to be conservative, no tradition is impervious to change. This kilim has a design of stylised carnations which can be traced back to the Ottoman court style, in fashion some two centuries before it was made. In the interval the carnation has been transformed into a typical tribal-style design consisting of a bold repeating pattern in different colour combinations. Nineteenth century.*
307 × 182 cm.
Neil Winterbottom.

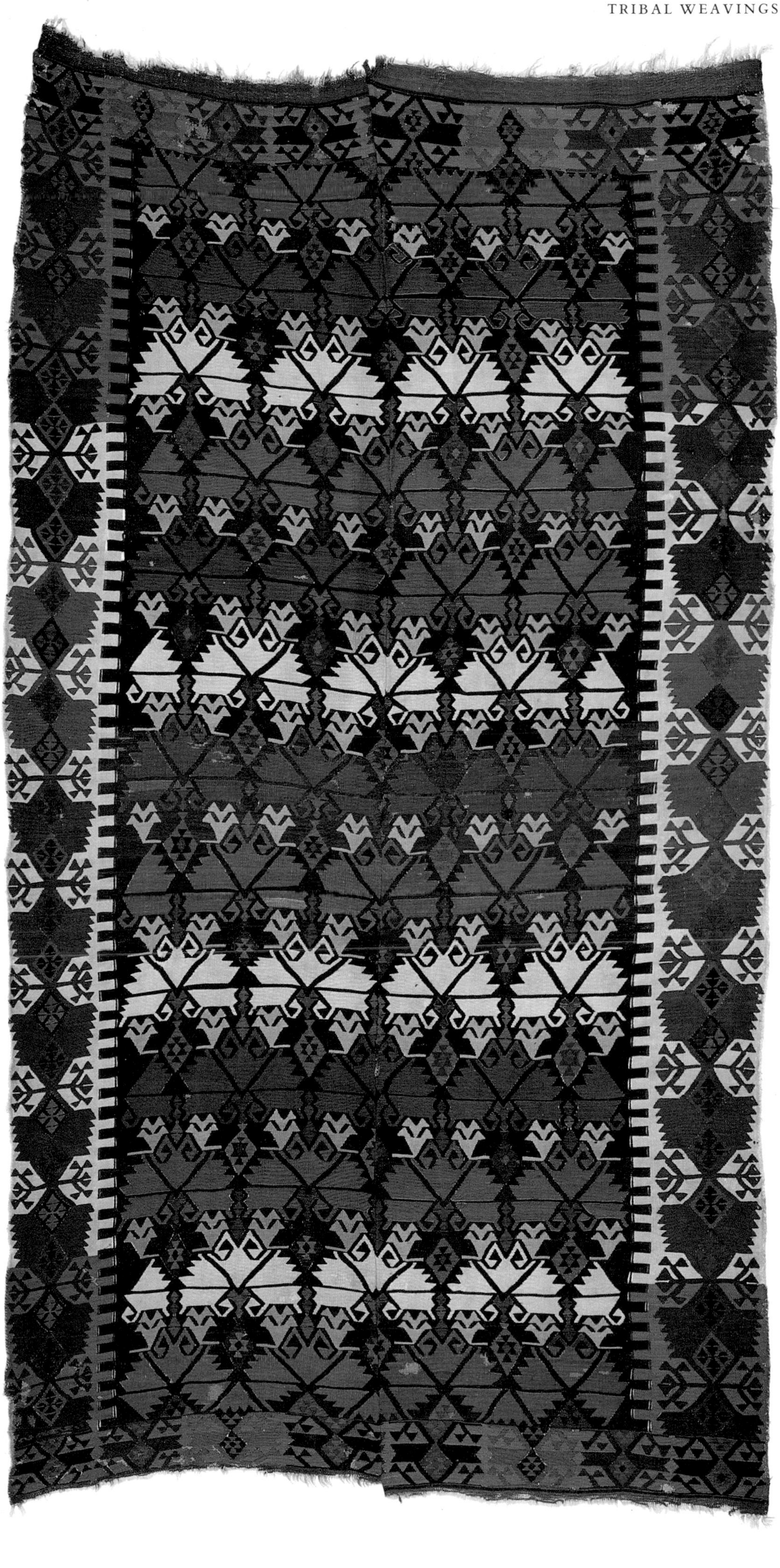

plant annual crops but migrate with their flocks. Yet others live in houses in the winter and tents in the summer within the same village compound. Lastly many are purely settled, with a self-contained life-style of tribal character.

From the carpet point of view these nomadic or village-based groups were, if not now, primary producers of wool and the source of many of the tribal carpets found in the market place today.

The nomadic life

When discussing tribal carpets, the nomadic tribes invariably come to mind first. It is easy to be romantic about the wide open spaces, the wonderful scenery and the self-sufficient life-style enjoyed by many of the pastoral nomads, while overlooking the extremes of climate, the ceaseless work and the ever present possibility of sudden poverty if livestock are lost in a hard winter or an epidemic.

The nomadic life-style has a long history. The technical advances in animal husbandry and the development of suitable light-weight, portable housing seem to have occurred in the third millennium BC. Once the breakthrough had been made the great Asian steppe was populated by a variety of unrelated groups of diverse ethnic origins sharing a common life-style and, at times, common religious and artistic conventions. Historical and archaeological evidence indicates that the life-style of the early steppe nomads 2400 years ago is very similar to that of the present-day steppe-dwellers such as the Mongols, Kazakh, Kirghiz, Uzbegs and Turkmen. There is an uncanny resemblance between the artefacts found in the famous frozen tomb of a nomadic chieftain at Pazyryk in the Altai mountains of Siberia, dating from around 400 BC, and those of the Kazakh people of today.[7] Apart from the adaptation of tent design to the local climate and conditions these nomadic groups maintain a way of life which is basically extremely conservative.

The nomadic life may have romantic appeal for western city-dwellers but it clearly also has a very real attraction for its long-standing adherents who continue to cling to it with extraordinary tenacity in the face of ceaseless suppression. Historically the more independent

LEFT: *One of the most exciting recent 'discoveries' is the artistic quality of Turkish flatwoven rugs or kilims. This ancient weaving tradition existed in Asia Minor long before the arrival of the Turks around AD 1000. As domestic weavings they tend to be conservative in design and are noted for their bold large-scale abstract patterns. Nineteenth century.*
416 × 160 cm.
Georgie Wolton.

RIGHT: *Until recently this type of kilim was unknown in the west. Their makers, the Yuncu tribe from Balikesir in western Turkey, consider them to have sacred and magical significance and are reluctant to part with them. When this is the case the appearance of such weavings on the market usually follows a weakening of tribal traditions. With the Yuncu it is probably no more than an erosion of old ways of thought brought about by prolonged contact with western influence. Nineteenth century.* 277 × 133 cm.
David Black Oriental Carpets.

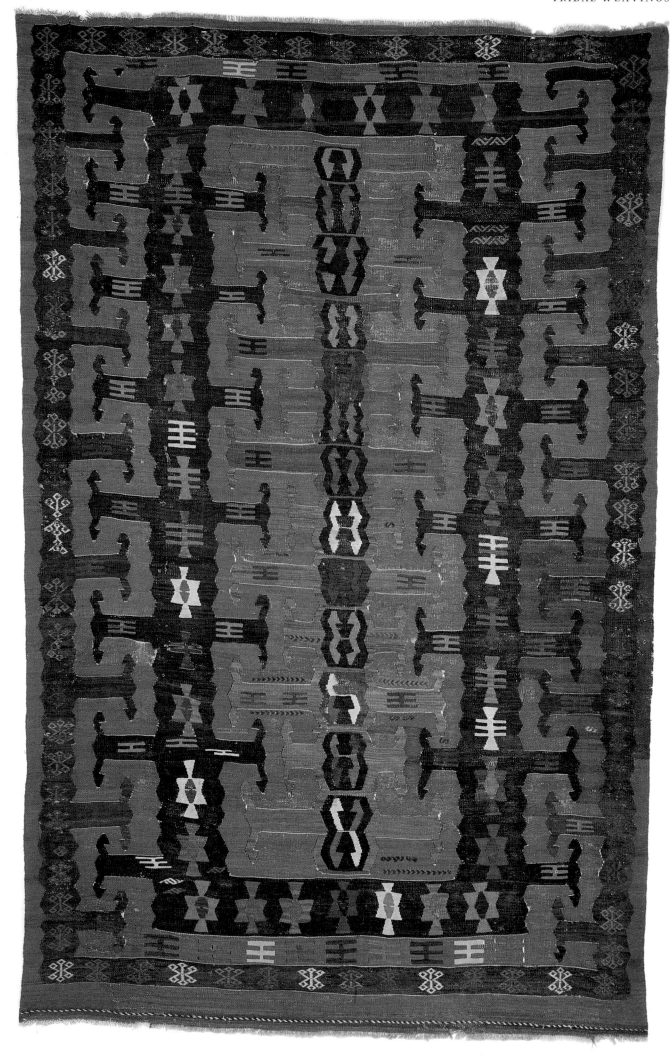

tribes have always been seen by central government as a potential threat and have tended to suffer as a consequence. In Persia in the first half of the eighteenth century Nadir Shah forcibly relocated several tribes on the periphery of his territory to act as buffers against potential invaders, though forcible suppression has been a commoner fate. The last hundred years has been a difficult time for the nomadic tribes. Some survive intact, others cling precariously to their old way of life, but within this period many have succumbed to superior forces and vanished.

For three decades the Russian authorities tried to convert the Kazakh nomads to the orthodoxy of fixed housing and agriculture. In spite of the liquidation and expulsion of 'reactionary' leaders, collectivisation, 'land reform' and 'livestock reform' – in effect a programme of confiscation and redistribution – and a fall in the number of sheep and goats to 10 per cent and horses to 5 per cent of their former numbers, the Kazakh way of life survives. The huge losses of livestock, capricious rainfall and the marginal nature of much of the steppe grazing land has forced those in authority to adopt a more flexible attitude to nomadism. Camel breeding programmes have now been launched and the nomadic family has been restyled as a 'brigade'. As an acknowledgement of the validity of the nomadic life, the 'red tents', housing adult educational activities, have joined the nomadic encampments.

LEFT: *This Turkmen rug has the typical shape, size and lower panel of tent door rugs, but not the characteristic design (see illus. p.91). The apparently complex field pattern consists of a fairly simple unit of design in horizontal rows. In succeeding rows the design inclines to the left and to the right alternately. This departure from the traditional door rug form is a reflection of the settled state and greater receptivity to outside influences of its makers, the Ersari tribe. Russian Turkeston, nineteenth century.* 187 × 120 cm.
Private collection.

A Kirghiz family cleaning the tent. They are shaking out a floor rug which is curved to fit the shape of the tent. It is made out of coloured pieces of felt which are cut out and sewn together in bold patterns. Rolled up above the entrance is a door rug of similar construction. The Turkmen in former times used a piled rug for this purpose (illus. p.76 opposite). Afghanistan.

LEFT: *The Shahsavan tribe is best known for its pileless weavings, especially small bags, which have usually lost their backs on their way to the west. The square faces of these bags are delicately brocaded in the weft wrapping (Soumak) technique which gives great clarity to their varied and interesting designs. Their flat surface makes them well suited to display on a wall and as a result have become popular as an inexpensive alternative to abstract paintings.* 46 × 46 cm.
Thornborough Galleries.

BELOW: *A distant view of an encampment of the nomadic Shahsavan tribe on Mount Savalan, north-west Persia. The woollen felts covering the tents are white when new and darken with age. They are replaced every five or six years.*

RIGHT: *The Shahsavan, a confederation of Turkic tribes in north-west Persia, are known in the west for their attractive pileless (weft-wrapped) saddle bags and horse covers. It is not known for certain what sort of piled carpets they wove, but this piece, probably made before 1880, could be one of them. It has, in common with their known weavings, stylistic features which relate it to Turkey, Persia and the Caucasus, and in appearance is almost certainly of tribal origin.* 427 × 142 cm.
Alexander Juran and Co.

A similar educational programme in Iran during the last twenty years, intended as a peaceable means of reforming the thinking and life-style of the nomads, has had the curious result that the Qashgai, a resourceful people, now provide the universities of Iran with more than their fair share of scientists and university professors, while members of their families still retain their pastoral way of life. The Turkmen of what is now Turkmenistan have not done so well. The defeat of the czarist Russian army by the Tekke tribe brought a crushing reprisal at the battle of Gok Tepe in 1881, the culmination of several decades of action against the Turkmen, from which the Tekke never recovered as an independent nomadic group. Large numbers fled to Afghanistan and Persia and many of those that remained changed from pastoralists into cotton farmers.

Many people have the idea that nomads wander about because they are unable to do any better for themselves and think of them as scruffy, impoverished loafers camping by the roadside with a few goats and chickens. The exact opposite is the case. Nomads, in order to pursue their way of life successfully, require a fairly high level of material wealth. They must have the apparatus for living – tents, felts, ropes, bedding, cooking utensils and so on – which is costly by itself and requires horses and camels for its transportation, and they must have livestock which provide meat, milk, leather and wool. The real wealth of the pastoralists lies in the size of their flocks and their holdings of livestock. When a community reaches a certain level of poverty, the nomadic life-style is no longer possible.

As a general rule nomadic groups prosper when central government is weak. In times of strong central government, they tend to suffer, and those on the poverty line are obliged to settle. Their seasonal migration between two sets of pasture is the most efficient use of marginal land yet devised, and settlement means that livestock can only be supported for part of the year; extinction is a matter of time. When the power of central government declines some groups may be able to revert to nomadism, as has happened in Persia recently with the Shahsavan tribe.

Tribal breakdown

It might be imagined that the energetic activity of local buyers in the nineteenth century, described earlier, would have sought out and perhaps cleared out every single carpet from the remotest tribal sources. This was far from the case. Some tribal groups have hardly been influenced by the changes of the twentieth century and have continued to produce work of full tribal significance, and a few, such as the Yuncu tribe of western Turkey, who considered their weavings to have sacred or magical properties, resisted the attempts of outsiders to obtain them.[8] Such people have sometimes been forced to sell under extreme economic pressure resulting from famine, war, or political manipulation. When this happens jewellery, carpets, needlework, anything that can be, is sold and so dispersed. Suddenly there is a brief flood of goods onto the market, which dries up equally quickly as the stock is exhausted. This has happened many times in the last hundred years with different groups, the last recently in Afghanistan when a mass of Turkmen tribal goods appeared in the market place.

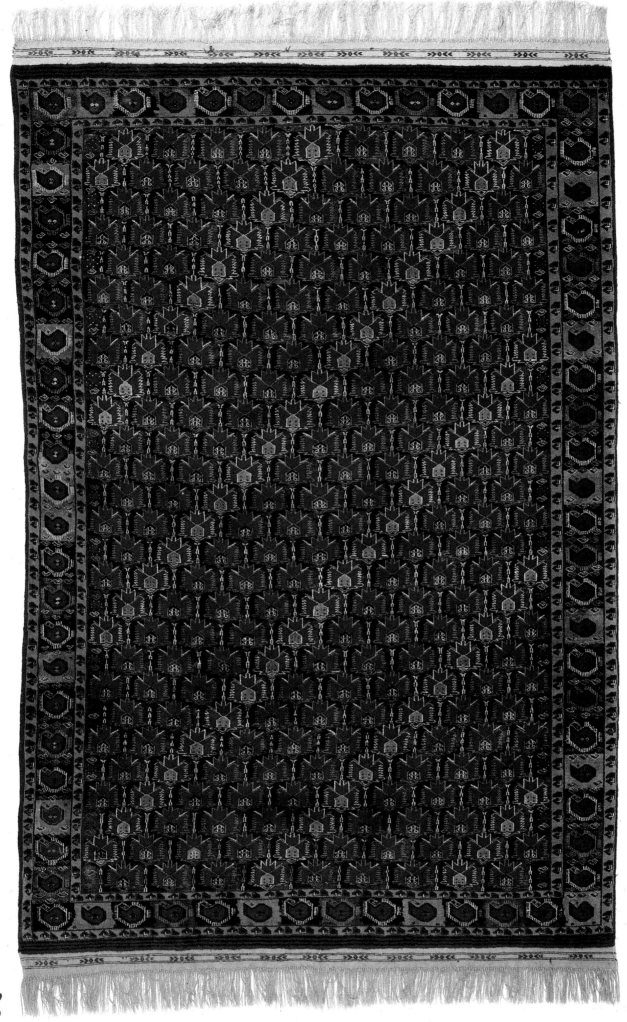

LEFT: *Recently a cottage industry in Russian Turkestan has begun successfully to reproduce old designs current in the last century when the Emir of Bukhara was ruler of the land. This carpet has a design used by settled Ersaris consisting of an endless repeat of leaf-like motifs on a ground of varying colour.* 270 × 183 cm.
L. Kelaty Ltd.

Sheep are all-important in the life of the nomad. Pakistan.

Evening milking time at a Kirghiz encampment.

The summer camp of the nomadic Shahsavan tribe is set up in the high pastures of Mount Savalan. On the right is their typical flying-saucer shaped tent. In the centre a less costly type of shelter is being erected consisting of a tunnel-shaped frame which will be covered with felt.

After such a catastrophe some tribes revive, but others are reduced to a level of poverty from which they never recover and are absorbed, dispersed, simply die out, or are forced to change their life-style from sheep herding to cotton farming, for example. In any event many of the tribal groups weaving in the early nineteenth century no longer exist. The recent arrival in Istanbul of a virtually unknown type of domestic weaving from the Konya area of Turkey presumably heralds the decay of such a local tradition. Uzbeg rugs of a particularly interesting type (illus. p.11) have recently come out of Afghanistan and one wonders what may be happening to their tent dwelling makers who inhabit some of the remotest parts of the world.[9]

The character of tribal weaving

The best way to appreciate tribal weaving is to understand its character. A carpet is made knot by knot, line by line, across its width, beginning from one end. It is possible to record every knot of the pattern on paper as a sequence of signs, one for each colour: two red, six blue, one black, ten white and so on. Carpet patterns written down in this way are called talims and are commonly used in workshops. The advantage of the talim is that it enables a weaver to execute a complex pattern without the higher weaving skill of being able to work in detail from an exact cartoon. A tribal weaver has to have the

equivalent of a talim in her mind. Remembering a large complex pattern is comparable to knowing by heart a complete orchestral score. Remarkable feats of memorisation are on record but the average weaver has an average mind and patterns cannot be too extensive. The way the tribal weaver gets round the problem is to learn a fairly large number of small patterns and use them in a variety of combinations and colours. The advantage of this is best understood in terms of telephone numbers. It is easier to remember twenty or thirty seven-figure numbers than six or seven numbers of thirty figures. Tribal weavings therefore tend to have repeating patterns of fairly small size. Without the mind-engaging quality of complex patterns, expressive power in tribal weavings is achieved through the use of colour, space and proportion, and when the best wool is used the added dimension of texture makes it hard to resist touching them.

Many people believe that the use of repeating patterns is the sign of a feeble imagination. The opposite is true. After many years of looking at tribal carpets I am certain the weavers knew exactly what they were doing; how much space to give a pattern or how wide to make the borders in relation to the field. The lack of this understanding is immediately apparent in copies of carpets of tribal design made after the loss of the tradition. Once a feeling for the tribal style of colour and spacing is acquired they become immensely exciting.

BELOW LEFT: *A boy is weaving a carpet in a Turkmen design, known also as the Bukhara pattern, in a Pakistani workshop. He has not yet learned the pattern by heart so he is consulting his piece of paper, written in special notation like a knitting pattern, called a talim. The talim records the sequence of colours in each row of knots.*

BELOW: *The tribal style evident in this weaving is reminiscent of the Turkic design tradition and may well derive from a different stream to most Turkish kilims. Nineteenth century.* 155 × 88 cm.
Mr and Mrs Paul Beck.

BELOW: *The tribal weaver can make interesting patterns out of quite simple elements. Here the camel motif is repeated in different colour combinations to create a charming effect. The use of a single main motif means the pattern can be memorised quite easily. The little animals in between are improvised as weaving proceeds. Around 1900.* 300 × 200 cm.
Jane Oundjian.

The decline of tribal weaving

The best of the tribal carpets which came to the west in the nineteenth century, in the first flush of public enthusiasm, have a vigour and clarity in their design, a quality of colour and workmanship lacking in later tribal work. The time when carpets were first sought out for export coincides with the beginning of a gradual downhill slide in tribal fortunes, and artistic achievement. In terms of carpet weaving we are observers of the very end of an ancient art form. The interest taken by the west in tribal weavings during the nineteenth century played a part in the lamentable decline which followed. Fortunately enough examples survive from the period prior to significant contact with Europe for us to have an idea of the vigour and quality of tribal weaving at its best (illus. p.5), and were it not for those early examples we might have an altogether different view of tribal carpet art. So consistent is the downward drift in standards that it can be used as a method of sequential dating. It did not, of course, happen overnight in every household. The rate varied considerably in different geographical areas; in some districts the decline occurred within as little as two decades while in some remote areas traditional standards have been maintained into the middle of the twentieth century.[10]

Asking why these changes occurred raises questions beyond the scope of this enquiry. Instead we will look at the circumstances of the decline to see what actually happened. Of course the problem of rapid decline is by no means peculiar to carpets. Similar changes have taken place and are still occurring in any number of traditional art forms throughout the world.

There were many influences in the second half of the nineteenth century bringing about change in the world

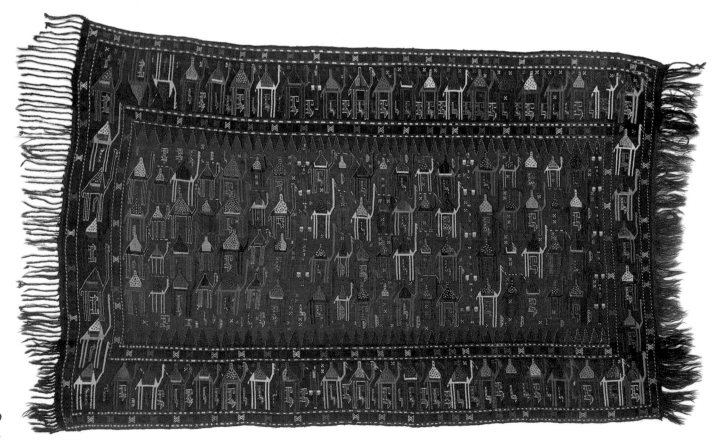

Kilims or flatweaves are used both as covers and hangings in the home. The powerful abstract designs of Turkish kilims have only recently attracted attention, and as yet little is known about them. As they are made primarily for use in the home they are classed with the tribal and domestic weavings. Konya district, nineteenth century. 370 × 150 cm.
Georgie Wolton.

of carpets, most of them arising from the increasing economic and cultural domination of Europe, America and Russia. Technology, industrialisation and new farming methods had a general erosive effect on the rural communities. Tribal and village life in Asia has been no exception to the rule that, wherever western cultural influences are felt, the traditional and indigenous culture tends to fade away. The influence of western culture was gradual, introducing new methods of transport, improved communications and different habits of living. Changes also occurred in people's expectations. Drift of the population from the land to the cities began but did not become a torrent until the middle of the twentieth century. There was also a general move against certain sections of the population which accelerated the decline. Nomadism in particular, as we have seen, was considered undesirable and to be discouraged by every means possible.

The introduction of synthetic dyes in the 1860s was a particular misfortune for the carpet makers.[11] While the dyers of today can achieve excellent colours, fast to light and washing, with a variety of fabrics, the results with the early synthetic dyes were far from happy. Rapid fading, running colours and a harsh discordant tone were the more obvious problems. In retrospect it is difficult to understand the sequence of causes and effects which led to what appears to have been a loss of colour sense among so many rural weavers in the late nineteenth century. Many have assumed that the corruption of traditional taste was caused by the dyes themselves, but this seems to be an over-simplified explanation for what occurred. In the beginning only small quantities of synthetic dye were used, as highlights, adding touches of colour to little details in the design. One has the impression that the new colours were used not because they were cheap but because they were a novelty. Cost may not have favoured the adoption of the new colours in the beginning, but the introduction of dyes that were easier to use probably facilitated the acceptance of new colours once the new dyes had acquired a price advantage over traditional ones. I should point out here that because nomads have been observed dyeing their own wool it cannot be assumed that they have always done so. This is in fact unlikely. Indigo dyeing, a comparatively high technology, was usually practised and maintained as a craft in towns and villages, trade secrets being passed from one generation to the next within families. The high standards of dye technology in former times, and incidentally the existence of local colour styles, were probably the result of nomads and villagers taking their prepared wool to these professional dyers.

To say that standards declined raises the difficult question of the validity of making aesthetic judgements from our twentieth-century viewpoint on the weavers of a hundred years ago. It is almost a function of getting older to complain of falling standards in the younger generation, so many claims can be discounted on the grounds that the elderly simply dislike change and regard it as decline. Again preference for colour is a matter of personal taste, even more so preference for colour combinations. But the changes that occurred in the wool dyes, and the resulting appearance of the carpets are more fundamental than a passing phase of taste. Indeed many later tribal and village weavings show an astonishing

LEFT: *The black goat hair tent is adapted for use in a hot climate. Livestock provide food, the material for shelter and clothing, and is the main source of wealth for the nomad.*

The field of this south Caucasian carpet is decorated with a traditional design used also by tribal weavers in Turkey, Persia and Turkestan. The use of small, easily remembered patterns in a repeat with different colour combinations is a typical device of the tribal weaver and gives this example a strong tribal character. It belongs to the Kazak or Genje group of weavings. Caucasus, nineteenth century 188 × 143 cm. **J. L. Arditti.**

RIGHT: *Many of the nomadic (Yuruk) tribes of southern and central Turkey share a common ancestry with the Turkmen of central Asia, a relationship often visible in their designs. The large indented ornaments in the field of this rug resemble the Turkmen gul patterns but are interpreted in a typically Turkish colour scheme and with a vigour of expression typical of Turkish carpets in general. Nineteenth century.*
264 × 132 cm.
Richard Lannowe Hall.

A nomad (Yuruk) of the Sachikara tribe makes sure his ram is well fed while on migration. Marash province, Turkey.

Interior of a house showing storage bags and bedding. Gaziantep province, Turkey.

Strong colours and vigorous designs contribute to the appeal of the weavings of the Ersari tribe, a group of settled and semi-nomadic Turkmen in Russian Turkestan and Afghanistan. This is the face of a large bag. Nineteenth century. 97 × 133 cm.
Private collection.

BOTTOM: *A good example of a tribal weaving which could easily be overlooked by someone unfamiliar with carpets is this incomplete strip, originally a shallow Turkmen bag. When this piece surfaced it was recognised by a collector as a hitherto unknown design, the work of the Salor tribe, which barely survived a military defeat in the 1850s. Nineteenth century.* 35 × 97 cm.
Private collection.

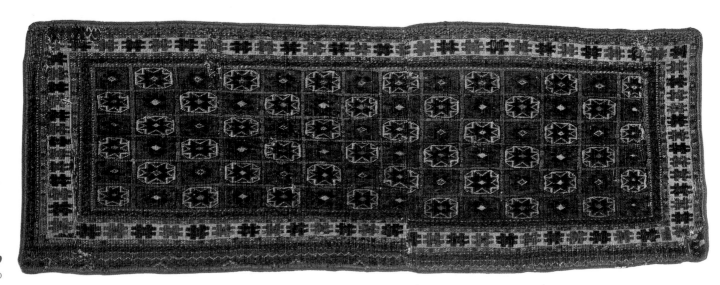

In the last century the Turkmen used a piled carpet for the door of the tent (see p.77) but the custom lapsed around a hundred years ago. This example, made perhaps 150 years ago is one of the loveliest examples of the work of the Turkmen Ersari tribe. 157 × 137 cm.
Private collection.   Photo: Lefevre & Partners.

The use of trappings by the Turkmen to decorate the bridal camel has already been mentioned (p.62). This example, with its design of birds within a lattice is the work of the Tekke tribe. This rare type does not appear to have been made since the 1880s, and there are only two examples in western museums, both acquired in the 1980s. 99 × 146 cm.
Private collection.

RIGHT: *The Qashqai are skilled copyists. The pattern of this carpet has been copied from a Persian workshop carpet of the early nineteenth century. Such copies are themselves copied, the design becoming progressively more angular and distorted each time. This carpet is so close to the original that were it not for the unmistakable Qashqai colour style, some hesitancy in the curves, and an interruption in the rhythm of the main border design at one end, it could easily be taken for a workshop product. The presence of silk in the foundation and the excellent workmanship indicate that the weavers were aiming to produce a carpet of the highest quality. Nineteenth century.*
318 × 171 cm.
David Black Oriental Carpets.

RIGHT: *No one is certain of the function of this little weaving. Such pieces are believed to have been used to decorate the entrance to the covered litter in which the Turkmen bride travelled to her wedding. It is Tekke work and must date from the mid nineteenth century.* 45 × 78 cm.
Private collection.

Two women getting the pattern sorted out. Love of bright colours and brilliant effect is evident in their clothing and in their choice of yarns for their weaving. The pink is almost luminous. Bechkan village, Gaziantep province, Turkey.

BELOW: *The profusion of camels and other animals in this flatwoven cover create a joyous effect. It is hard to believe that this is worked entirely from memory. It was made in a little-known area on the border between Turkey, Persia and the Caucasus.* 210 × 200 cm.
Fritz Langauer of Adil Besim OHG, Vienna.

apparent loss of the sense of colour and form, and it would be easy to convince the sceptic that the dull, muddy, faded and running colours of some synthetically dyed rural weavings around the turn of the century are nothing short of a calamity.

The question of the harsh and clashing colours we see in later rural weaving is more difficult to judge. In rural communities today, for instance it is common to find textiles worked in colours of the brightest, most luminous hues available, including yarns with glaring fluorescent dyes. Here one has to remember that the weavers have always preferred the clearest and brightest hues, so this is nothing new. These combinations may be harsh and clashing to our eyes but it seems to bear out the idea that the raw preference of the weavers was for brilliance of effect. As a corollary it should be mentioned that it is practically universal that children and those with an uneducated or unprejudiced taste prefer clear bright colours to dull muddy ones.

The changes we are discussing are intimately tied up with what the weaver thought and felt about the object she was making. The main pressure on the tribal weaver was not sale and export but making things for the home and special occasions, with the chance of some surplus if time permitted. Everything had to be functional as well as decorative. Some pieces, such as those made for a wedding were highly important for the weaver and had a significance rooted in the traditions and expectations of the whole community. As long as community life retained its old rhythms the weaver was eager to give everything to the task in hand, which was to make something precious and beautiful for the adornment of the home and the honouring of guests. Therefore the declining standards we are discussing reflect a fundamental change in the whole fabric of community life.

Major changes in a tribal weaving tradition over a short period of time generally mean that the women are no longer weaving for themselves but for the market. They have become part of a cottage industry. This is not to say there is anything wrong in selling one's handicraft, rather the period of changeover is one of difficulty and confusion. For example, the carpets produced by the generation immediately following the defeat and forcible settlement of the Tekke tribe in Turkestan are finely worked but show increasing decorative elaboration and confusion of the traditional patterns. It is as if some restraining hand had been removed leaving the weavers free to add more and more to the pattern in an attempt to make it attractive. It was no longer their peers who were scrutinising their work but some imagined public. The tribal society no longer nurtured and gave meaning to their weaving, it was the necessity to earn money. At first they wove their usual bags and pouches but they changed rapidly, departing further and further from the usual sizes, shapes and traditional patterns. The need to weave for money was a direct consequence of the dissolution of tribal society, which in turn was mirrored in the change in their weavings.

From a collector's viewpoint the dominance of commercial pressures leads to the production of articles which as tribal artefacts are meaningless and insignificant. To be significant today a tribal rug must have been charged with significance by its maker and her society at the time it was made.

LEFT: *The shape and size of this Turkmen carpet is close to the traditional long, narrow shapes made in the cottage industries of Persia. Its dramatic character and vibrant colours are typical of Ersari work so it may well have been made by a group long settled on the banks of the Oxus who had abandoned their tents and were perhaps on the way to becoming a cottage industry. Russian Turkestan, nineteenth century.* 312 × 178 cm.
A. S. Crosby.

RIGHT: *The nomadic Bakhtiyari tribe, which undertakes the most arduous seasonal migration of any tribe, are well known for their carpets but only recently has their rich tradition of pileless weaving become known in the west. This kilim, if not actually woven by them, shows strong Bakhtiyari influence.* 508 × 137 cm.
Georgie Wolton.

LEFT: *Long described as 'Caucasian', these striking pileless weavings are now believed to be the work of the Shahsavan tribe which used to migrate across what is now the border between Iran and the Azerbaijan SSR. They are also called Verneh, a Russian term for the weaving technique.*
200 × 150 cm.
L. Kelaty Ltd.

RIGHT: *This little rug, a celebration of horsemanship, has an inscription with a message of blessing and good luck, typically said to someone getting married. It therefore presumably also celebrates a wedding. Fars district of south Persia, possibly Afshari work. Nineteenth century. Approx. 75 × 35 cm.*
Dr J. C. Hardy.

BELOW: *This typical tribal weaving was originally the decorated face of a storage bag, one of a number hung on the wall of a Turkmen tent and used to contain personal effects such as clothing. The pattern is ancient and has a powerful simplicity. Part of its visual effect is the result of a peculiar Asiatic design concept in which the border acts as a window onto a portion of an endlessly repeating design. The disappearance of the design beneath the border, which at first sight looks strange to the western eye, is the means whereby this idea is conveyed. The artistic awareness and highly developed sense of colour evident in this piece, the heritage of a tribe of pastoral nomads, is handed on from mother to daughter. Salor tribe. Nineteenth century. 79 × 127 cm.*
Private collection.

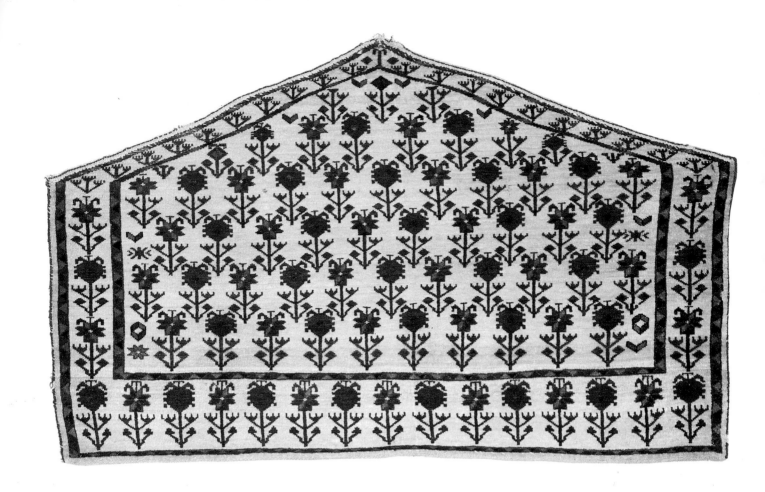

ABOVE: *Among the Turkmen it is the custom for the bride to ride to her wedding in a covered litter on a camel decorated with trappings she has made specially for the occasion. Naturally she devotes great care to making things for such an important event and the best Turkmen work is to be found in items made for the wedding tent and procession. Five-sided trappings are used in pairs to decorate the flanks of the camel. This is the only known example of Saryk workmanship. White is the colour for weddings among the Turkmen and the white ground blotched with red is associated in many cultures with the idea of fecundity in marriage. Nineteenth century. 84 × 135 cm.*
Private collection.

A woman of the Suleiman Kheil clan, a nomadic group from Afghanistan.

RIGHT: *Such pieces are made by nomadic Baluchis in Afghanistan and north-east Persia. The dark colours are a speciality of the tribe and it should be pointed out that it is more costly and difficult to produce dark blue than light blue. The colouring has therefore been chosen intentionally. As a work of art this example has a wonderful grandeur and dignity and to be appreciated must be seen in daylight. Twentieth century. 279 × 165 cm.*
The Rug Shop.

Chapter four

The cottage industry

It was in the sand-buried ruins of east Turkestan (Sinkiang) that Sir Aurel Stein found scraps of piled carpet dating from the sixth to the ninth century. Carpet making continues in the region today. This example from the oasis of Khotan has a design of a pomegranate growing out of a vase at each end of the field, an ancient motif conveying the idea of life and plenty. The older carpets, of which this is a good example, have soft lustrous wool and harmonious colours derived from natural dyes. Synthetic dyes were adopted rather early in this region, during the 1860s and 1870s. Nineteenth century. 374 × 200 cm. **Wher collection.**

Organisation

In the cottage industry the weavings are by definition for sale. The advantages of having a loom at home are obvious: weaving can be fitted in at any convenient moment, and an eye can still be kept on the children. The women are in effect taking on part-time self-employment to increase the family income. Raw materials can be obtained in a variety of ways. The family may have its own sheep; alternatively village women may buy woollen yarn direct from neighbouring producers, often local tribal people, or from the bazaar. Wool bought in the bazaar is likely to be of inferior quality and is often 'skin wool', that scraped from hides before tanning. The wool and the cost of having it dyed may represent a capital outlay which a poor villager can barely afford, especially as it may take three months or more to complete the carpet, sell it to a merchant and get the money. Instead of buying the materials herself the cottage weaver may obtain ready dyed yarn from a contractor who pays the weaver on delivery of the completed carpet. This system appears to have been introduced into Persia in the second half of the nineteenth century but has a longer history in Turkey. The arrangement allows the contractor to exercise a direct influence on the type and quality of work by specifying the size, colour, fineness and pattern. The main drawback is that no agent or buyer can possibly supervise the work of hundreds of separate looms so there is no effective quality control. In this respect the cottage industry differs markedly from workshop production where quality control is a critical factor in successful marketing.

The cottage industry system is fairly responsive to the demands of the market place. When the market is flourishing more looms are set up and more hours devoted to weaving. The cottage weaver is always on the look-out for new ideas. Successful patterns are copied and learned and new ones tried out. Sometimes sample carpets are made to show a selection of field and border patterns, or a new design such as bunches of flowers (illus. p.104), which, at the time it was made, must have been adapted from a European textile pattern and considered suitable for the European market. With the help of such a sample an order could be placed, the client specifying the size and which field and border patterns he wanted.

Cottage weaving is long established. In the seventeenth and eighteenth centuries many rugs were exported to Europe from western Turkey from this source. Large numbers of these survive in churches in the Transylvanian district of Rumania (illus. p.105). They are small and woven in a typical cottage industry style much as the rugs of the Milas district were in the nineteenth century and are still today.(illus. p.148). One feature of this style is that many of the designs are rustic

BELOW: *The adaptability and inventiveness of weavers in the cottage industry is illustrated by this carpet. It is a complete piece, not a fragment, and has been woven as a sample for a client who may be thinking of placing an order. It shows what a field pattern looks like and what borders can be chosen to go with it. The design in the field, with its bunches of flowers and wreaths, has been copied from a European textile pattern and was presumably thought to be suitable for a European client. Bijar, north-west Persia, nineteenth century.* 152 × 152 cm. **Private collection.**

RIGHT: *During the seventeenth century a cottage industry in western Turkey successfully supplied the export market with small, attractively coloured rugs with patterns based on the Ottoman court style. They appear in American and European painting and survive in fairly large numbers in Italy, Hungary and Rumania. There was a custom at this time, in the Transylvanian district of Rumania, for merchants to give gifts of Turkish carpets to the local church, where many are still to be seen. Turkey, seventeenth century (often referred to as 'Transylvanian').* 177 × 117 cm. **Wher collection.**

versions of earlier more sophisticated patterns (illus. p.154), particularly those in vogue in the Ottoman court.

An interesting parallel occurred around the same time in the Caucasus, then under Persian rule, where circumstances never seem to have been suitable for the establishment of court-quality workshops such as existed elsewhere in Persia. Instead there was a flourishing cottage industry making adaptations of Persian designs on looms not more than two and a half metres wide (just over 8 feet), about the maximum for cottage weavers but often exceeded in the technically more advanced workshops supplying the courts. Although the patterns are clearly based on complex and sophisticated originals, in the hands of the Caucasian cottage weavers the carpets are coarsely though sturdily woven, all the graceful curves have been changed into a succession of straight lines and angles, and the colours have an unsophisticated primary character. They include the well-known dragon carpets (illus. p.107 opposite), which are believed to be based on Persian originals, although no Persian carpets in this design are known. They were evidently made in large numbers and successfully marketed abroad. Many survive in Turkish mosques and they even reached Europe, as paintings of the period reveal.

The strongly individual, local character of these Turkish and Caucasian weavings is typical of the cottage industries in general which tend to become concentrated in definite areas with a definite style in each. The local identity of a style is maintained not by policy but as the natural result of children learning from their parents and grandparents. Regional accents and dialects are maintained the same way; the style of speech acquired in childhood persists throughout life; likewise children learning to weave do so in the style of those around them. Communal weaving styles are observed to be remarkably constant over several generations and serve as the main guide in determining the source of a carpet. As already mentioned the dyeing of the wool is often handed over to specialised dyers. If everyone takes their wool to the same few dyers, this will give some uniformity to the colours used in the area and tend to reinforce the consistency of the local style.

Before contract work became common, cottage weavers would have a small repertoire of patterns peculiar to the village or locality, and every community would have its own characteristic weaving technique, colour style and patterns. The growth of the contract system has meant that what the weaver produces today is more often determined by the policy of central buyers than by local tradition. This is particularly so in Turkey where in theory some degree of official control is exercised over all commercial looms. If a cottage industry becomes highly organised, to the point that all weavers are under contract to a single agent and all are using cartoons supplied by the contractor, who incidentally may supply the loom as well, then there is little to distinguish this set-up from a commercial workshop. These are the kind of conditions found in Kayseri, Turkey, and in a large part of Pakistan's production.

Some workshops allow weavers to work at home. For example, at Hereke, where the most technically advanced carpets in Turkey are produced, a highly skilled weaver who has worked for years in the workshop may elect to work away from the hurly-burly of the shop floor in a

RIGHT: *The cottage industry has a long history in the Caucasus. In the seventeenth century Caucasian weavers were making rustic versions of Persian workshop carpets. This dragon carpet, with its primary colours and angular rendering of curves, is a typical example. The term 'dragon' refers to the stylised S-shaped dragons in the design which can be identified by reference to other carpets. It is believed that the design originated in a Persian workshop, but no Persian carpet with this design is known. 469 × 223 cm.*
Keir collection.
Exhibited: *The Arts of Islam*, Hayward Gallery, London 1976. *Dragon rugs, a Loan Exhibition*, Textile Museum, Washington D.C. 1948.

A woman weaving a carpet at home using a cartoon with a medallion design she has bought in the local market. The simple upright loom has few technical refinements. The warps are kept under tension by wedges above the lower beam. Bijar, north-west Persia.

RIGHT: *What later became the huge production of Saruk began as a cottage industry. The early examples, made before weavers had learned to use detailed cartoons, have an attractive slightly rustic quality compared to the more refined later pieces. This prayer rug may well be one of the carpets which in the early days helped Saruk to gain its great reputation. 193 × 132 cm. Shaikh and Son.*

local cottage. In this case all that has happened is that some work has been decentralised from the main workshop; the weaver has not suddenly become a worker in the cottage industry. The same applies in some Persian towns, such as Qom, where weaving is actually carried out at home but the superior technical quality of the work, the use of original cartoons from a central design studio and the quality control make the finished carpet indistinguishable from a workshop product.

The style of cottage industry carpets

Since carpets are woven for sale weavers must always be prepared to learn new patterns. One way of doing this is to copy another rug knot for knot. This is a common practice and it can be very confusing to find a pattern typical of a particular region woven in unusual colours. The give-away is always the weaving technique which is usually sufficiently distinctive to pinpoint the origin.

Another way is to work from a cartoon, a skill developed by the more specialised workshop employees and not usually possessed by the average housewife weaver. The most she would be able to do is to follow a drawing of a design to get the general shape and spacing and fill in the details by eye. For example she might have a drawing of a section of the border or part of the field pattern and use this as a guide to her weaving without following it knot for knot. In doing so she is faced with two main problems and her solution to them gives cottage-made carpets their characteristic appearance. First is the problem of how to make graded curves. She is quite able to produce curves of a sort, but they tend to progress in fits and starts, with straight bits and angles throughout. The minutely graded elegantly swirling lines of the workshop carpets are replaced by irregular, somewhat clumsy, angular curves. Second is the problem of how to make neat corners in the border. Borders normally have a rhythmical, alternating pattern which repeats all the way round the carpet. At the corners designers prefer to make a neat transition by placing a motif in each corner, at exactly forty-five degrees, so that the border design changes direction smoothly. The cottage weaver (and this applies also to the tribal weaver) may start off by managing to place motifs neatly in each corner but she is unlikely to be able to do the same when she comes to the transition between the side borders and the end border (illus. p.46). Only a border worked from a cartoon continues uninterruptedly round all the corners. It is interesting to examine the finely worked Qashgai carpet (illus. p.93) to see if the border, which at first sight seems to have 'corner solutions' (meaning that it was worked out by a designer before weaving started) actually goes right round the carpet without a break in its rhythm.

Some cottage weavers have the unusual skill of being able to 'compose' a complete carpet from a simple sketch. Cecil Edwards, who travelled extensively throughout Persia in the 1930s, relates an amusing incident which occurred in the Heriz area. One day he noticed an interesting carpet being woven in a house and when he inquired about the pattern the weaver showed him a handkerchief printed in two colours in Manchester with a floral border and medallion with corner pieces. She had used this as the basis for weaving a full-sized carpet in twelve colours. All the curves, being too difficult to copy

LEFT: *Tabriz, a major weaving centre in Persia, is represented by this delightful carpet, with its plain field enlivened with sprigs of flowers. It was in Tabriz that the first of the modern carpet workshops was set up in the 1870s. This carpet, made for the Persian market, was woven before the establishment of these workshops, and, like the Khorasan carpet (illus. p.61), has something of the character of a cottage product. Nineteenth century. 570 × 270 cm.*
A. Zadah, Persian Carpets.

RIGHT: *The village of Ladik in western Turkey is best known for its prayer rugs (illus. p.154), but among the earlier weavings are a number of rare and attractive long narrow rugs with a design of conjoined medallions decorated with stylised tulips. Around 1800. 340 × 117 cm.*
Eskenazi, Milan.

Many Kazak rugs have patterns derived from those brought westwards by the migration of the Turks. The design of this Kazak is of different origin. It retains a single element of a large and complex Persian design of the seventeenth century, which in the intervening years has been modified by the cottage weavers and turned into something interesting in itself. It is variously known as the 'sunburst', 'eagle' and 'Chelaberd' design. Nineteenth century. 196 × 142 cm.
Lord Dufferin.

exactly, had become angular, in the typical cottage manner.

To summarise, weavings made within a cottage industry tend to have strong primary colours and bold emphatic designs; their patterns often incline towards the sophisticated but in execution always retain an element of the rustic, and in style exhibit a distinct local character.

Local traditions

Before discussing the more technically advanced workshop carpets some comment must be made on local traditions, although the output of individual villages and districts are too numerous to describe in detail.

The Caucasus is an area rich in both carpets and mysteries. Very little dependable information is available for this remarkable part of the world, a mountainous district containing a profusion of ethnic minorities, each with its own character and language, where problems of origin and history, such as that of the Basques of the Pyrenees, are repeated many times over. The Caucasus has a long history of cottage production and exportation which continues today. Most of the output from the region has the typical character of cottage work and is named according to the village, town or district of origin. Many designs can be traced in an unbroken succession of transformations back to modified Persian patterns of the seventeenth century. Some weavings have a strong tribal character (illus. p.87) and resemble the weavings of tribal groups in Turkey and Persia, and those of the Turkmen of central Asia. As no one is certain who made them they are difficult to classify. The sensitivity of the cottage industry to new ideas and influences is well illustrated by the Caucasian weavers who were among the first to introduce European design in the form of a field pattern decorated with cabbage roses in the 1840s and among the first to use synthetic dyes in the 1870s.

In Turkey the cottage industry system was established long ago and is so deeply embedded in rural life that truly tribal carpets are few and far between. In addition to carpet weaving there is a vigorous and extremely ancient indigenous tradition of kilim, or pileless weaving, which has attracted serious attention only recently. Pileless weaving is a domestic craft and flat-woven items are used for every conceivable purpose. They have been classified as tribal weavings.

Not much is known of Persian cottage weaving before the nineteenth century as little reached the west, but occasional datable carpets give evidence of a vigorous and diverse industry. In the first half of the nineteenth century carpet production in Persia had fallen to a low level, but the cottage industry, charmingly described by one Persian dealer as a 'side job' never ceased. Once stimulated by foreign demand Persian village women responded energetically and output increased enormously. Demand reached such a point late in the nineteenth century that western engineers were stimulated to try and invent a machine for making knotted pile carpets. This was achieved in 1910 by the British firm of Tomkinson who obtained a patent from Renard Frères of Nonancourt, France, for a loom based on the Jacquard principle. Initially the Tomkinson carpets imitated the popular red and blue Turkey carpets but they were never very lucrative and they had difficulty in competing with the weavers of Hamadan

LEFT: *This Kazak carpet has what is known as the Karachop design, an ancient pattern found both in Caucasian and Turkish carpets. Its bold abstraction has made it and other Kazak carpets popular as a focus of interest in the modern home. Nineteenth century.* 225 × 170 cm.
Avakian Oriental Carpets Ltd.

The Sevan design, another of the range of Kazak types, is well seen in this example. It has the long shaggy pile and strong colours so typical of Kazak rugs. A related form of its field pattern is also found in Turkish carpets. Nineteenth century. 220 × 183 cm.
Avakian Oriental Carpets Ltd.

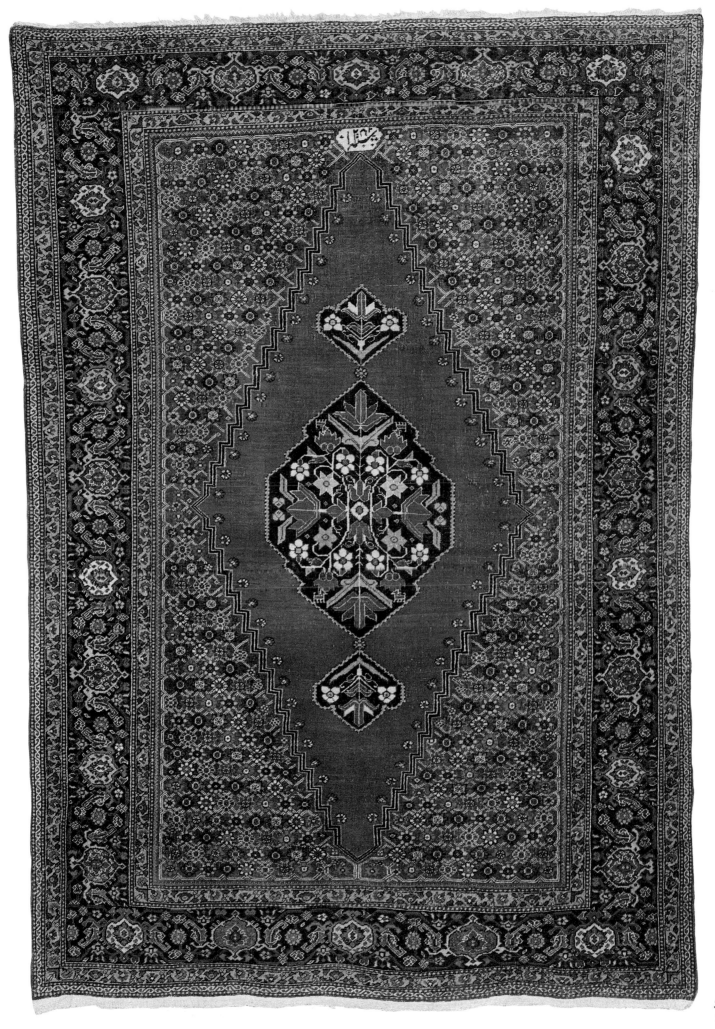

PREVIOUS PAGE LEFT: *Kazak rugs from the Caucasus are noted for their strong individual character and have been given names by Russian scholars according to design and place of origin. This Borchaly design is one of the few in which the border and field are given equal emphasis. Nineteenth century. 221 × 155 cm.*
Eric Bradley collection.

PREVIOUS PAGE RIGHT: *This carpet, a typical product of the Farahan district of central Persia, is dated 1282 (AD 1865). Such carpets were special favourites of the older generation of dealers born in the Middle East. They are now rarely seen and the characteristic Farahan style of weaving seems to have died out around the turn of the century. The design in the main border proceeds in regular rhythm along the sides and ends, but changes abruptly at the corners. This is a typical feature of the cottage industry style. 196 × 130 cm.*
Private collection.

Kurdish weavers in the village of Kelardasht making a carpet on a vertical loom. As weaving proceeds they gradually raise the bench.

RIGHT: *For as long as anyone can remember a hardy group of Kurds in the village of Kelardasht has woven carpets of a distinctive robust type on fixed upright looms set up against one wall of the house. As weaving proceeds they raise the bench they sit on, which in the end is level with the roof. Many centres of the cottage industry ceased weaving altogether in the 1940s and 1950s but not that of Kelardasht which continues to this day. 1930s. 216 × 109 cm.*
Simon Boosey.

A well-dressed horse in Kurdestan, north-west Persia. The horse cover is now in the Royal Scottish Museum, Edinburgh.

ABOVE: *In the early decades of this century there was a cottage industry in the little village of Bakhshayesh near Heriz in north-west Persia which became renowned for its well made carpets with soft colours and bold patterns. They have an appeal which has not diminished in the light of changing fashions. It is only to be regretted that such rugs have not been made in the last forty years. Nineteenth century.* 300 × 235 cm.

Eskenazi, Milan.

RIGHT: *Kurdish weavers are the makers of one of the best known types of all Persian carpets. The town of Senneh, the capital of Persian Kurdestan, has become world famous for its fine rugs and carpets, which have a unique construction and colouring. These carpets, the product of one of the most refined cottage industries in Persia, have nothing in common with the Kurdish tribal weavings (illus. p.39) made in the tents and tribal villages of mountainous Kurdestan. This rug with the Vekilli design has the soft colours and typical weave of Senneh work. Nineteenth century.* 184 × 130 cm.

Atlantic Bay Carpets.

LEFT: *Even though the major part of the output of a village was sold, a few pieces must have been made for domestic purposes. This carpet has the style and character of a product of the cottage industry in the Farahan district. It appears to be a betrothal rug, so it could have been woven as a special order or alternatively it may have been woven to celebrate a marriage in the weaver's family. Nineteenth century. 397 × 197 cm.*
Joseph Lavian.

Turkey has a long and noble tradition of prayer rugs. In Persia, with a few notable exceptions, they are a nineteenth-century phenomenon and the same applies in the Caucasus. This attractive Caucasian prayer rug bears a colloquial tribal name, Chi Chi, but it is almost certainly a product of the cottage industry. Nineteenth century. 152 × 117 cm.
Robert Attenborough.

who could work practically as fast and more cheaply. Latterly the looms came to be used for specialised orders such as the making of a carpet bearing an insignia to fill a particular space. The last Tomkinson machine-knotted carpets were woven in 1962.

Some products of the cottage industry in Persia are known throughout the world, such as the carpets of Bijar, famous for their clear colours and durability; those of Senneh for their fine workmanship and pastel colours; and the weavings of the settled Baluchis in Khorasan for their dark colours, lovely wool and economical price. Some extremely handsome carpets were made in villages populated by settled people mainly of Bakhtiyari origin. Technical and craft standards in the past were at a high level and have remained so (illus. p.47). They managed in the nineteenth century to make some huge carpets which were never formally designed but followed a style of pattern woven in Jowshaqan, which has been unfailingly popular in Persia for centuries.

The textile department of the faculty of fine arts at Marmara University, Istanbul, are behind a most interesting social and economic project in the field of carpets. A number of villages in western Turkey are inhabited by settled (formerly Turkmen tribal) people with a long tradition of carpet weaving, certainly brought from central Asia in their westward migration over 500 years ago. Within the last century commercial pressures and synthetic dyes have combined to cause a sad deterioration in the appearance of carpets woven in these villages. The project is to persuade the weavers in these villages to return to using traditional dyes and materials and to assist the villagers within local cottage industries to form marketing cooperatives. The results have been unexpectedly successful. The women have never forgotten their traditional patterns and with a little assistance from carpets borrowed from the local mosque (often dyed with hideous synthetic colours), they have been able to continue in the manner of 100 years ago. Now it is as if the last century of weaving had never existed. The colours, using only natural dyes, are bright (as they should be) and the patterns astonishing for their traditional consistency. Careful marketing allows weavers to sell at a reasonable price yet obtain more than they were getting for contract work, and as a result standards are rising. Made by Fatma Yagli, Budaklar village, Ayvacik district. 230 × 150 cm.

Dobag Project, Textile Department, Faculty ⟨of⟩ ⟨fi⟩ne Arts, Marmara University, Istanbul.

LEFT: *The popularity of Caucasian rugs in the west has prompted entrepreneurs in Turkey to get weavers in the cottage industry to produce rugs of Caucasian character and design. They are inexpensive compared to the Caucasian originals and are very much better than an earlier generation of insipid copies, made in the 1920s and 1930s, known as Pergam by the trade. This rug is modelled on a rare type of Caucasian prayer rug from the early nineteenth century (cf. illus. p.123). Edremit, north-west Turkey.* 174 × 110 cm.
Moutafian and Co. Ltd.

This rug from the Caucasus embodies all the typical features of Kazak work: lustrous wool, long shaggy pile, strong colours and a bold pattern. It has the interesting distinction of having been published in one of the early books on carpets by Mumford in 1900. It also illustrates the 'protective barrier' aspect of the border. The main border has a strong rhythmically alternating pattern and is flanked by two 'guard stripes' with a reciprocally interlocking design. Nineteenth century. 211 × 165 cm.
Private collection.

RIGHT: *Occasionally it can be extremely difficult to say where or by whom a rug was made. This beautifully woven rug has a pattern such as one might find in a Persian workshop carpet, but it is by no means typical, and some little details in the borders indicate that it was not worked from an exact cartoon. The crimson silk wefts and the silk warps in bands of different colour are an unusual feature and a clear indication that the weaver was aiming to produce something special. The design was probably copied from another valuable carpet. Nineteenth century.* 211 × 135 cm.
Baktiari Oriental Carpet Gallery, Arky and Ginger Robbins, San Francisco.

BELOW: *A little-known cottage industry flourished during the nineteenth century in what used to be called Chinese or east Turkestan, now the Sinkiang province of China. There is every indication that the tradition of carpet making in this district is very old. The population speak Uighur, a Turkic language, and although predominantly Muslim, the carpets preserve designs carried over from the Buddhist past of the area. Designs also include rustic interpretations of Chinese patterns such as this enchanting, if rather angular, version of a Chinese paeony scroll pattern. Around 1800.* 140 × 92 cm.
Wher collection.

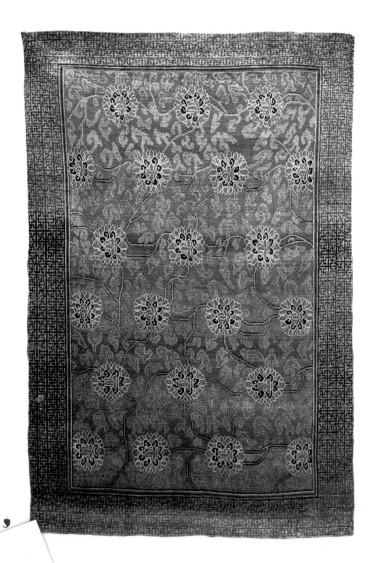

Chapter five

Workshop or town carpets

The workshop carpet is characterised by a balanced overall design (the work of a designer), perfectly graded curves, borders which progress evenly right round the carpet, faultless technique, and the avoidance of great expanses of primary colour. They are the product of advanced technology and a system of specialised production. This recently made example has an inscription knotted within the plain woven band at one end, 'Woven in Iran, Esfahan, by Serafian'. 233 × 149 cm. **Cyrus Carpets.**

The growth of commercial carpets

Tribal and cottage looms are seldom more than 8 feet wide. A carpet can be any length but its width cannot exceed that of the loom. In Persia people adapted the way they furnished their homes to what was available, and instead of having a large carpet covering the whole floor, the custom grew up of having a suite of four carpets in the main room. The traditional long narrow shapes of Persian carpets never found favour in the west and as carpets became more and more a normal part of home furnishing, people asked for much wider carpets for their living rooms. They also wanted colours and patterns which would fit in with their existing décor. These the trade could not easily supply because the massive looms required to make such carpets were beyond the technical resources of the cottage industries. Enterprising merchants therefore set about filling this gap in the market by providing capital for setting up workshops in Persia specifically organised to supply the needs of the western market. This phase, beginning around 1875, has been called the revival period. Carpet production grew rapidly and the export of Persian carpets became a huge business. Europeans also entered the scene to invest in production. The first factory financed and managed by Europeans was founded by Ziegler and Co. of Manchester in 1883.

The mid-nineteenth century had been a period of economic decline in Persia. Some weaving centres appear to have ceased production, but most of the old-established ones were active and were producing rugs, but not in any great quantity. Then suddenly this basically traditional craft, existing at several different levels of technical accomplishment and adjusted to local needs, was subjected to an unprecedented demand for export goods. The demand was met by increased output. During this period thousands of new looms went into production, in the cottage industry and in commercial workshops. The resulting output dominated the market, dwarfing the importance of the tribal rugs. The more remote tribal and village weavers, who normally worked to fill basic domestic needs while aiming to produce a surplus for trade and barter, also experienced the increased demand for carpets. They obligingly wove more rugs, but the increase was commonly accompanied by a decline in standards, although some tribal groups proved remarkably resilient. In the commercial workshops standards, far from declining, improved to reach a high level of technical excellence. But, as the term 'export goods' has come to imply in the larger field of art objects, aesthetic values changed. The commercial carpet industry created a new product which came to occupy a special place in the history of carpet art.

BELOW: *In commercial workshops designs are converted to cartoons by drawing them onto squared paper. These are cut into sections, pasted onto cardboard and coloured by hand. In this Rumanian factory cartoons for a European design are being prepared.*

RIGHT: *The south Persian city of Kerman has been an important centre for the production of workshop carpets back to the sixteenth century. Like many other centres Kerman suffered in the troubled times of the nineteenth century and weavers turned their hand to making shawls, a lucrative export business dominated by Kashmir. Shawls finally went out of fashion in the west about the time that demand for carpets was increasing sharply. The presence in the city of looms, skilled weavers and designers, enabled the Kermanis to take immediate advantage of the turn of events, since when skilful designers and the traditionally high standards in the workshops have taken Kerman to a position of world renown. This fine rug woven 'by the order of Hajj Muhammad Ibrahim Kermani' has a shawl design. Around 1900. 224 × 139 cm.*
Robert Franses.

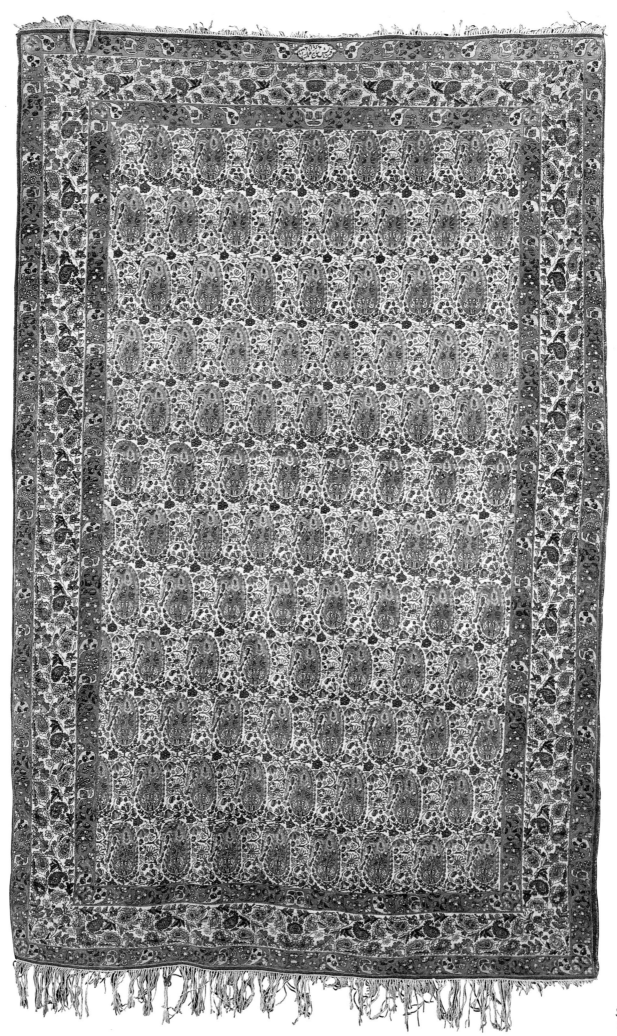

Recent disturbances in Iran have upset the normal flow of trade. Workshops in China, which are currently producing carpet of consistently high quality and have on their staff many talented designers, have turned their attention to filling the gap. After some uncertain starts there can be little doubt that the proverbially adaptable Chinese have mastered an unfamiliar field of design and are now making interesting woollen carpets in Persian designs. 137 × 84 cm.

L. Kelaty Ltd.

Production

The new system converted carpet making into a production process, which is continued in the same way today. Craftsmen are recruited, trained and employed by the company to work on each stage. These include the purchase of raw materials, sorting, carding and combing, spinning, plying, dyeing, designing, cartoon making, weaving, clipping and washing. Specialisation allows each craft to be developed to a higher level than is possible among the cottage and tribal weavers who do everything themselves apart from the dyeing. It also makes for a much more uniform quality in the finished article. On the other hand the weavers and spinners are no more than employees in a large organisation.

The workshop or town carpet as it is often called is almost by definition woven from a cartoon. The art of the carpet is therefore the art of the designer. The weaver reproduces the design with more or less accuracy according to her skill. Recognising a designed carpet is usually easy. The curves are graceful, flowing and even, the overall composition is perfectly balanced and the design flows evenly all round the border, with a motif neatly and exactly placed in each corner. Sometimes a tribal or cottage weaver will copy a workshop rug, the

Making large carpets of Ushak character at Sparta, Turkey, 1910. This is a type of 'low tech' workshop producing large quantities of coarsely made, crudely patterned carpeting.

Qashqai weavers, for instance, being excellent copyists (illus. p.93). (Although an astonishing feat of workmanship, a careful look at the curves and the corners reveal that the finer points were beyond her.)

The distinction between a cottage industry and a workshop is not always clear and some overlap does occur. I referred previously to the important weaving centre at Qom, which developed in the 1930s and which has no factory as such, all the looms being in the weavers' houses. The highly skilled weavers work under contract and weave to an exact design supplied to them by the contractor, who also supplies the yarns. The quality control is good and the end product has all the features of a workshop carpet. The carpets of Kashan are known today for their quality and workmanship but in the late nineteenth century, at the start of the revival, all carpets were woven on home-based looms. A glance at these early Kashans reveals the typical features of cottage carpets, clumsy corners and wonky curves in otherwise excellent products. As the weavers became more skilled and were able to reproduce exact patterns the carpets took on more of the character of workshop products.

At the other end of the scale one finds employees working in a factory making large but crude carpets, not woven from a cartoon. An example of this type of work are the 'Sparta' carpets, coarse imitations of earlier Ushak designs made in Isparta, Turkey, in the early decades of this century.

So far we have mainly discussed Persian workshops which, as they were first in the field, held a dominant position for many decades. But it was not long before market demand stimulated others to join in. Workshops for large-scale production were established in Turkey, Egypt, Pakistan and India, and later in Nepal, Rumania, Russia and Afghanistan; and on a smaller scale in many countries, among them Egypt, Tunisia, Israel, Lebanon, Yugoslavia and Iraq. In China there appears to be no indigenous folk tradition although carpet workshops have been in continuous production for at least three hundred years. With growing demand production was increased and China continues to maintain a huge export trade.

As with any commercial operation the product is governed almost entirely by what will sell. An exception is the occasional carpet made to order. What the public will buy depends on dozens of imponderable factors related to fashion, national prosperity, international politics, war, revolution and so on. A great advantage of the commercial workshops is that they can respond immediately to new fashions or requests from importers overseas, as illustrated by the Art Deco carpet made in China to a design presumably provided by a European (illus. p.142). Market demand was not all from overseas; the pictorial carpets for which Kashan is well known were clearly a Persian fashion. In the absence of specific requests the managers of the workshops, in consultation with the designers, have to make a policy decision on what designs to produce. Today, in the carpet producing countries of the world, there are few truly original schools and none that approaches the quality of work produced by the court designers of four hundred years ago.

RIGHT: *In the workshop the weaver is trained to work knot by knot from a cartoon and execute exactly what the designer specifies. It is thus possible to have any design woven into a carpet. Here the design is a picture drawn in the nineteenth-century Qajar style depicting Alexander the Great and his war with the devil. The work has been executed to a high standard and there is a large colour palette, including some synthetic dyes. Kashan, early twentieth century.* 201 × 134 cm.
Fairman Ltd.

Since the 1870s Persian designers have continued to produce good work. Some design studios are still active and original and manage to retain a traditional character; Qom carpets are a good example (illus. p.7). Chinese designers have successfully maintained their high standards of former times (illus. p.143). They have also tried their hand with new patterns. The European designs work well and are popular and their new Persian designs, although seemingly uncomfortable in the hands of a people who have nurtured the world's greatest designers, are improving rapidly. The Chinese understand better than anyone the use of space; in contrast Persian design is concerned with pattern and overall surface decoration. Tibetan carpets have designs with a strong individual character and are becoming increasingly popular (illus. p.139). Indian designers have tended to rework old Persian patterns. Apart from the Hereke factory (illus. p.14), few new ideas have come out of Turkey, although some carpets of the highest technical quality have been woven in Kum Kapu, a district in the old quarter of Istanbul, with designs based on classical Persian models (illus. p.112).

Since it is possible to translate more or less any design into a knotted pile carpet, designers today should take up the challenge and, following in the footsteps of a long line of designers before them, should apply themselves to making modern designs suitable for this ancient craft.

A carpet workshop in the Caucasus, 1913. Few people are aware that workshops were active in the Caucasus at this time.

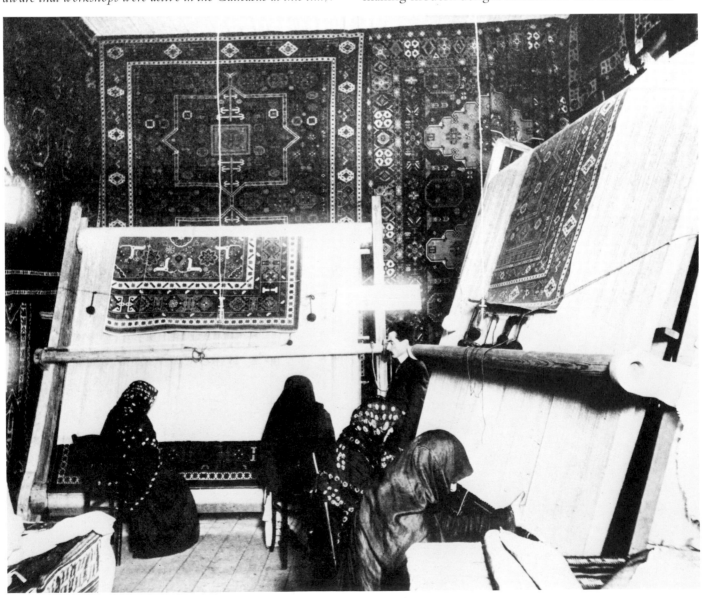

ABOVE: *This unusual carpet is complete in spite of its appearance. It was woven as a sample, showing what a particular field and border design look like. It was common for customers to place orders using such sample carpets. The pattern is loosely based on a seventeenth-century Persian design and is in the style of the first products of the factory set up in Arak, central Persia, by Ziegler and Co. in 1883. This type of piece is often called in the trade Mahal, a term used for some carpets woven in the Arak district.* 173 × 150 cm.

P. & O. Carpets Ltd.

RIGHT: *Newcomers to the big league of carpet manufacturers are the workshops in Nepal employing Tibetan refugees. They are made using a uniquely Tibetan weaving technique with wool of the highest quality. Their designs are original, yet typically Tibetan. They are not expensive and have recently become deservedly popular.* 201 × 146 cm.

OCM (London) Ltd.

In the 1920s the production of carpets in China expanded
enormously. It is not always appreciated that carpets have been
made in Chinese workshops since at least the seventeenth
century. Early pieces are as rare as they are interesting. This
rather tired example illustrates the Chinese designer's masterly
use of space and preference for a perfectly balanced composition.
In this respect the aesthetic approach of the Chinese designer is
in marked contrast to the Persian approach in which overall
surface decoration is important. Eighteenth century or earlier.
211 × 132 cm.
Private collection.

A carpet factory in Rumania.

140

ABOVE: *This carpet stands out from the crowd because of its extraordinary design and colouring. For a brief period Art Deco carpets were woven in China to European designs. This is such a piece and illustrates the point that in a workshop any design can be executed – an outstanding challenge for the modern designer. Around 1930. 298 × 240 cm.*

Dinolevi, Florence.

RIGHT: *The Chinese carpet export business collapsed in the 1940s but in recent years has grown steadily. Its success is based on quality control and the talent and inventiveness of its designers. The design of this silk carpet is based on that of earlier Chinese carpets and makes an interesting comparison with the one made some 250 years earlier (illus. p.141). 215 × 137 cm.*

OCM (London) Ltd.

RIGHT: *In the 1920s workshops were established in the Kum Kapu district in the old quarter of Istanbul for the manufacture of carpets of the very highest quality. These found a ready market and are highly prized today. Their designs, as in this example, were often based on sixteenth- and seventeenth-century Persian originals. The luxurious effect of this silk carpet is enhanced by the recessed areas within the main motifs which are brocaded with glittering precious metal filament. Twentieth century.* 310 × 210 cm.
L. Kelaty Ltd.

Turkish women weaving carpets from a cartoon. The workshop is equipped with wide looms which have many technical refinements. As weaving proceeds the carpet is wound onto the lower beam and the warps unwound from the upper. The metal rods are attached to a lever which prevents the upper beam from unwinding and keeps the warps under tension.

Chapter six

Court carpets

Background

Court carpets are so important historically that some discussion of them is necessary. In describing the events leading up to the establishment of the commercial workshops in the late nineteenth century, the impression may have been given that they were entirely new. It was only the scale of production which was new; true workshops directed towards the manufacture of large and technically advanced carpets had existed before. They were set up from time to time to serve the needs of the ruling courts, and a number of their remarkable products survive in museums, noble families, churches and the private collections of the wealthy. A brief look at the background to the establishment of these workshops helps towards a broader understanding of carpets as a whole.

Middle Asia has been invaded many times throughout history by the steppe nomads, tent dwelling pastoralists of the vast plains stretching from China to Hungary. The best-known incursion was that of the Mongol horde led by the much-feared Chingis Khan, in the twelfth century. Less well known are the earlier movements of the Turkmen or Turkoman nomads into central Asia beginning in the tenth century. In fact these two groups intermingled and between them had a profound influence on the art and culture of the Middle East. The reason for these huge migrations is not known with any certainty, but it could well have been as a result of competition for resources, or war, in which more easterly tribes forced their neighbours in a westerly direction. In these disturbed times powerful leaders emerged who welded separate tribal units into huge military confederations. The self-sufficient life-style, high mobility, high-powered bows of special construction and formidable horseback archery, gave the nomads an overwhelming military advantage in the field. Wherever they came, after the phase of destruction, the new conquerors contrived to become great patrons of the arts and learning, and their noble families sired a number of the major dynasties in the history of Asia, among them the Sefavids of Persia, the Ottomans of Turkey, the Mamluks of Egypt and the Mughals of India. ('Mughal' or 'Mogul' is a corruption of the word 'Mongol'.) Even after several generations in power the rulers of these great dynasties never really forgot their tent dwelling past. This is reflected in their liking for tented encampments, the cultivation of the hunt and the architecture of their tombs and palaces, which owe much in form and layout to the tent. It is also reflected in the cultivation of the knotted pile carpet, that very art form which served as the main medium of artistic expression for their ancestors the steppe nomads.

Court styles and their influence

The rulers of the great Islamic courts of the sixteenth and seventeenth centuries were notable for their patronage of the most outstanding artists of the day. An important element of their patronage was the maintenance of a design atelier under the immediate direction of the court. The court artists produced designs in a variety of media including textiles and carpets, setting the pace for new styles and fashions. The carpets therefore, together with ceramics, calligraphy, paintings and so on form part of the corpus of art produced under the patronage of the dynasty and are named accordingly. As the ruling houses were Muslim, the carpets are, with reason, classified as Islamic art. The workshops themselves were not usually under the direct control of the court but acted as suppliers of goods to the standards and specification required. Working for the court did not preclude the manufacturers from engaging in normal commercial activities; nor did it prevent rival workshops from turning out similar, less expensive items in the same style. For example a whole gradation of quality from the outstanding to the mediocre is seen in carpets and textiles worked in the Ottoman and Mughal court styles. High fashion then as now was surrounded by its imitators. More imitators copied the imitations and so the style worked its way outwards to towns and villages far from the capital. Women in the rural communities may never have seen the originals, and had no access to luxurious materials, so they copied the new style in the medium they were accustomed to. Velvets were translated into embroidery and knotted pile work; luxurious carpets with silk foundation were copied using less costly yarns. Inevitably the designs were adapted and corrupted but they lived on to be incorporated into the folk tradition. Here they survive in rustic form centuries after the originals have passed out of fashion. For a deeper understanding of later carpets in all the countries mentioned it is necessary to study the court carpets of earlier times, a task beyond the scope of this review.

The strongest supporters of the court styles were the weavers in the cottage industries. They kept their version of the styles going long enough to exert a strong influence on the character of the carpets made in the new commercial workshops when they were set up at the end of the nineteenth century. Designers naturally drew on the current vocabulary of ornament, and carpets of today are full of references to classical models.

In Turkey there was a vigorous domestic tradition even in the fifteenth century. Carpets evidently made in cottage industries were being exported to Europe time, as paintings of the period reveal. During th half of the sixteenth century a new prayer rug de

introduced with an architectural theme, featuring arches
supported by columns. Prayer rugs prior to the Ottoman
interpretation included the arched form but no columns.
Many have drawn attention to the strong symbolic
association between prayer and the idea of a gateway,
threshold or opening to another world. The lamp often
represented hanging from the apex of the arch indicates
that another idea is intended – that suggested by the verse
in the Koran, '*Allah is the light of the heavens and the earth ;
a likeness of his light is as a niche in which there is a lamp . . .*'
Also contained in the design is the idea of the mihrab, the
recess or arched plaque in the wall of a mosque orientated
towards Mecca and indicating the direction to pray. The
arched prayer design therefore has no single association
but includes some element of all these. Its reformulation
in the late sixteenth century has given Turkish weavers a
rich theme, which after three hundred years may now be
found in a great array of different interpretations.

Another style of luxury carpet was supplied to the
Ottoman court during the nineteenth century, probably
from a factory at Hereke set up in the 1860s.[12] They are
extremely finely knotted on a silk foundation with
interpretations of sixteenth-century Persian designs.
After early difficulties, including a fire, the Hereke
factory perfected its lavish carpets. When they appeared
in small numbers in the west they were initially mistaken
for weavings of the sixteenth century and have often
been published as such. With the lapse of the Ottoman
dynasty in 1918 Hereke carpets reached a wider public
and the factory now produces some of the finest
weavings on the market. The possible existence of carpets
made for the Ottoman court between the seventeenth
century and the 1860s has been overlooked by scholars
and it is still possible that some atypical carpets in the
Persian style were made in the eighteenth and early
nineteenth century. The large silk carpet (illus. p.150) has
the character of a piece made for the Ottoman court but
is unusual in that its design, instead of being in the Persian
manner, has been copied directly from a known
sixteenth-century Persian carpet in the Museum of Art
and Industry in Vienna. It may therefore have been made
in the 1920s after the publication of the Vienna carpet.

Persian court carpets are a study in themselves. Space
permits only a passing mention of this golden period.
Commercial establishments capable of producing carpets

LEFT : *The cottage industry still flourishes in Turkey in the
same places as it did in the seventeenth century, and with
related patterns. The village of Milas became well known in
the nineteenth century for small rugs with lovely colours,
particularly prayer rugs, of which this is a typical example.*
175 × 119 cm.
Richard Wright.

RIGHT : *The closest villagers could get to the luxurious velvets
and silks made for the court was to copy them in the materials
they had to hand. Through the ages luxury textiles have been
an important source of designs for the embroiderer and carpet
weaver. The design of this carpet fragment, a cottage-made
product from seventeenth-century Turkey, has been copied from
that of a contemporary velvet or brocade.* 278 × 108 cm.
Private collection.

This large silk carpet must have been made in a workshop equipped with technically advanced looms, highly skilled weavers, draughtsmen and cartoon makers. Technical details point to Turkey as the source. Only the workshop at Hereke, patronised by the Ottoman court, or the workshops in the Kum Kapu quarter of Istanbul were sufficiently advanced to have woven such a piece. As it is a copy of a sixteenth-century carpet in the Museum of Art and Industry in Vienna, which was first published in 1926, it is most likely to have been woven in Istanbul in the 1920s. 617 × 310 cm.

L. Kelaty Ltd.

of court quality existed in Kashan, Isfahan, Kerman, Tabriz, and in some centre in Khurasan, probably Mashhad. Herat, now part of Afghanistan but historically linked with the culture of Persia and the central Asian region of Transoxiana, may also have been a centre. There are likely to have been other centres and some may have nurtured more than one establishment producing separate types of carpet. The great contribution made by Persia to the world of carpets is the medallion design, perhaps best known in the famous Ardabil carpet in the Victoria and Albert Museum. Like many artistic ideas the central medallion theme is an old one with ancient religious and metaphysical roots. It consists basically of a centrally placed, more or less circular design of crenellated outline, placed on a field covered with swirling tracery. In the Persian carpet it found new expression and continues to this day as the most popular and widely used of all carpet designs. The early carpets

have exerted an indelible influence on the whole character of Persian commercial design, including that of the cottage industry, and even extending to some tribal carpets.

The Caucasus does not appear to have been the home of workshops capable of producing court-quality carpets. Glorious carpets were made from the seventeenth century onwards and large numbers exported, but they have the character of cottage industry work.

India has no long-standing indigenous tradition of woollen, knotted pile carpets. Court-quality carpets were made from the second half of the sixteenth century, initially with a Persian character but later in a uniquely Mughal style. In the middle of the seventeenth century they reached an astonishing peak of incomparable technical and artistic perfection. The foundation is silk and the pile worked in the wool of the mountain goat of Tibet and Ladakh which has the dyeing and wearing

properties of wool but the visual and tactile character of silk. No carpets made since have surpassed the sumptuous effect of the carpets made during the reigns of Shah Jahan and Aurangzeb in the seventeenth century.

Workshops continued shakily into the nineteenth century when they were joined by the Indian jails in an expanding production. Contrary to the tradition in most other countries the carpets are woven mainly by men.

The workshops which supplied the courts are therefore a special case in the history of carpet art. They produced the most technically accomplished, sumptuous and visually prodigious carpets ever made and did so in response to the demands of the court, and the continual supply of money. The system of court patronage is not so different to that between customer and commercial workshop, and it can be likened to an extreme form of commercial development. The ruler is simply the main customer and the main market force.

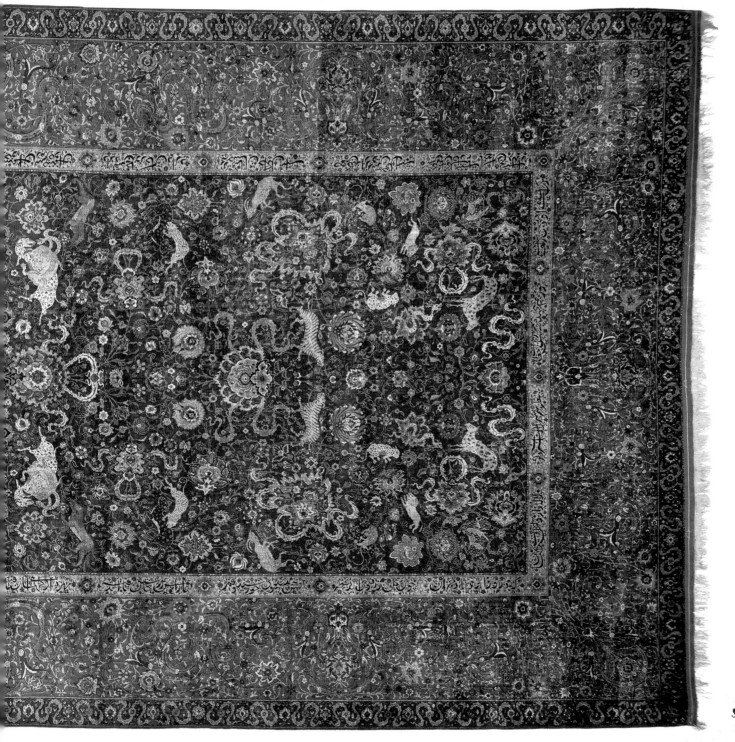

152

LEFT: *Designs emanating from the court workshops have had a powerful and sustained influence over the last 400 years and, spreading far beyond their point of origin, remain the biggest single influence on the design of commercial carpets. This recently made, part silk Chinese carpet successfully captures the Persian court style.* 137 × 76 cm.
L. Kelaty Ltd.

ABOVE: *In this (incomplete) seventeenth-century carpet Turkish weavers in a cottage industry have translated the design of a luxury velvet into that of a carpet. This is how designs emanating from the court found their way into village weavings. Some, such as the Ottoman prayer design, lived on for centuries, others, such as this one, had a shorter life.* 281 × 218 cm.
Wher collection. Photo: Lefevre & Partners.

154

Chapter seven

Symbolism

The form of this Turkish prayer rug, made in the first half of the nineteenth century, derives from the design of luxurious carpets made around 1600 for the Ottoman rulers. It has been kept alive by weavers in cottage industries all over Turkey. This rug is from Ladik, a town in central Turkey which supplied many pieces to the overseas market in the nineteenth century. It is interpreted in the bright clear colours they favour. 190 × 112 cm.
Marshall Wolf.

The idea of symbolism

Everybody is intrigued to know what all the different designs and motifs found in oriental carpets mean and it would be a pleasure for me to be able to give some examples of different designs together with a statement of their meaning – a sort of A equals B explanation. Unfortunately symbolism is not amenable to this kind of treatment and the numbers of books there are, each with a different explanation of the symbols, is a testimony to the difficulties involved. The subject seems to encourage fantasy and speculation of a special kind. Each author has built up in his mind a set of explanations of the symbols corresponding to his own particular view of life, and as time passes has grown more and more convinced of their correctness. In the end they are the truth for him. Thus it is that at the moment there are a hundred and one indubitable truths to explain any one motif.

The idea of the symbolic is not easy to grasp, especially for the western mentality, which favours the formal and literal approach and finds difficulty with the metaphorical and allegorical. The literal approach can demolish the metaphorical, make it look ridiculous and at the same time miss its message entirely. It reduces the symbol to a sign. If a motif has a single generally accepted 'meaning' then in common parlance it becomes a sign – this stands for that in a one to one relationship, as in musical and mathematical notation, traffic lights, road signs, the printed word and so on. The symbol, in the sense we wish to use it, cannot be substituted for by a word; rather it addresses in a language peculiar to itself a part of the mind which does not use words. Were it not so there would be no value in using any form of communication other than words. Music is a prime example of a rich experience not enhanced by verbal descriptions. The powerful evocation of feeling through the sense of smell is a raw example of direct communication without words. Colour can have the same effect. By themselves these stimuli are simple and unorganised, but in a work of art at its highest level they are organised to convey information directly, by-passing the use of words. The information can be a feeling, an aspiration, an evocation, a reminder, a wish, a prayer, a longing, an offering or any or none of these things.

But what symbolic difference is there between peasant and court weaving? What about a rug woven by a humble, illiterate, uneducated peasant? Was she fashioning an object 'intended to convey meaning?' In symbolic content, in ability to formulate a coherent message, the peasant's rug cannot be compared for example with a court rug woven in Sefavid Persia under the influence of a Sufi school of mystical ideas, but nevertheless it has something to say. The weaver had thoughts and feelings, and was much more aware than we are of the presence of unseen and uncontrollable forces threatening to bring sickness, death or misfortune. She had her hopes and aspirations and strove to make her work appealing to those who would look at it. Certainly you can be sure her work is full of deeply felt meaning and conveys many messages in the motifs she used for protection, good fortune, long life and so on. Nevertheless there is a difference between the work of the two sources. The different symbolic content of the two examples is analogous to the difference in their artistic categories. On the one hand the careful design of the court carpet is worked out in every detail and includes a conscious symbolism. On the other the peasant rug has a pattern learned by heart and worked from memory. Some motifs will have a clearly understood meaning for the weaver, but others will be in altered or diluted form symbolic motifs from a more conscious source in the past, perhaps originally a court atelier, which rural weavers have made their own and continue to use, aware the design is important but with no idea of its original significance. Indeed they may have acquired a new meaning quite detached from their original significance.

To give an example, it is believed that an esoteric school of thought was influential in shaping the design of some Sefavid carpets. The central medallion design, traceable back to ancient China, was refashioned by the court designers in a mystical Islamic context around the idea of the ruler as the centre and axis both of the world and of the faith, and the theme of the gateway to heaven.[13] The rural weaver using a medallion design is unlikely to be aware of all its historical and mystical associations. Again the main border with its two minor borders or 'guard stripes' is also used in a conscious fashion in the same Sefavid carpets as the delimitation of a sacred enclosure, guarding and protecting what is within from harmful outside influences. This function of the border to create a place apart, a protected space, was and is, in contrast, very well known to tribal and rural weavers.

Old and new patterns

Learning something about the origin of a pattern may help to reveal more of its symbolic significance, if any. For instance one Caucasian carpet pattern is believed to have been copied from the design printed on a packet of needles imported from the west, another from nineteenth-century European textiles patterned with bouquets of roses. Border designs may appear as field designs and vice versa. Tribal weavers frequently copy luxury textiles designed in workshops, such as velvets or brocades. In these examples symbolic content is minimal. In some tribal weavings the main designs are characteristic of one particular clan or sub-tribe. Many of these are extremely old and have a deep cultic significance rooted in the remote past. It is my belief that many of the repeating rounded designs of the Turkmen can be traced to an origin in the Buddhist eight-petalled lotus and have therefore been carried on from a period of time before the coming of Islam to central Asia, when the region was predominantly Buddhist.[14] Other patterns may belong to a much older layer of belief, having their source in respect for totemic animals or birds. There is a constant motifs in and out of the vocabulary of every community. The importance of Islamic artistic he primarily Muslim countries of the Middle

East has already been mentioned. In Turkey the prayer design is particularly important and in Persia it is the preoccupation with the overall decoration of entire surfaces.

Finally, generally speaking it is unwise to read too much into the symbolism of carpet designs, just as one does not on the whole look for symbolism in music except in special cases. It is better simply to approach carpets, like music, in a receptive frame of mind. Then the various styles will find their echo in different observers. It is my own wish that some of the older tribal and cottage weavings, which include works of abstract art of a high order, will be spotted and recognised for what they are by a larger public.

'Because the eye can in a moment encompass the whole surface of a rug it is assumed that it can be seen at a glance. But no worthy piece gives up its meaning so lightly. Its inner beauty is revealed only to a sympathetic and leisurely observation which knows how to read the pattern. The finer examples are often as elaborately composed as a symphony and as sensitively organised as a sonnet. The elements of the design are like notes in a melody or words in a poem: only as they are individually understood, interpreted and assembled is their meaning made plain. In order to see a rug, therefore, it is necessary to sense the quality of each component part, to feel the manifold relations of the parts to each other and to comprehend them all in a harmonious and significant unity. The great carpets are ready to declare their glory, and a wonderful glory it is, to those and only those who will make this effort of attention.'

A. U. Pope, 1926.

Carpets have been made at various times in Morocco, Algeria, Tunisia and Egypt. At first sight this may look like a Chinese carpet but in construction and wool quality it is quite different. The design appears to be derived from an early medieval Egyptian textile pattern and the little brocaded band at each end is reminiscent of some north African work. This rare and attractive carpet was probably made in north Africa, but where is uncertain. 229 × 156 cm.
Paul Nels.

Footnotes

1. Holm, Bill, *Northwest Coast Indian Art, An Analysis of Form*, University of Washington, Seattle and London 1965.
2. My favourite is the Gapylyk tribe, the alleged name of a main Turkmen tribe. 'Gapylyk', the Turkmen name of a lambrequin hung over the doorway inside the tent, was assumed to be a tribal name when the term was transliterated from Russian. In: Franses, Jack, *Tribal Rugs from Afghanistan and Turkestan*, London 1973, p.7.
3. Technically indigosulphonic acid, a light blue-green dye obtained from indigo by treatment with sulphuric acid was the first synthetic dye. It came into use in the 1840s but the major development in synthetic dyes was in the 1870s and 1880s.
4. In technical achievement the Pazyryk carpet can be compared to a product of the cottage industry. It has no corner solutions and was not worked from a cartoon. It consists of a system of repeats with variations that would be within the competence of a highly skilled tribal weaver. On balance I believe it was not woven by those that buried it.
5. The revised dating of the so-called Seljuk carpets has been well and forcefully argued long ago by A. Geijer in *Ars Orientalis V*, Michigan 1963, but her views have largely been ignored and the carpets continue to be published as 'Seljuk'. They are typical cottage industry products based on the design of costly silks from China, just as the two seventeenth-century Turkish fragments in this book are based on silk velvet or brocade designs made for the Ottoman court.
6. See Yetkin, Serare, *Early Turkish Carpets*, Istanbul 1981, plate 76.
7. See Rudenko, S. I., *Frozen Tombs of Siberia, The Pazyryk Burials of Iron Age Horsemen*, London 1970.
8. See Acar, Belkis in Landreau A. et al., *Yörük*, Museum of Art, Carnegie Institute, Pittsburgh 1978, p.27.
9. The origin of these weavings I have taken on trust from those who are in a position to know; see O'Bannon, G. W., *Kazakh and Uzbeg Rugs from Afghanistan*, Pittsburgh 1979. He believes they are made by house dwellers.
10. Sometimes weaving standards are retained while dyeing standards fall. Very few people in middle Asia still use the full range of natural dyes.
11. See note 3.
12. The Ottoman dynasty flourished in the eighteenth and nineteenth centuries and the court certainly patronised carpet workshops. Where these were prior to 1860 and what they made is still being worked out.
13. See Ettinghausen, R., 'The Boston Hunting Carpet in Historical Perspective', *Boston Museum Bulletin*, vol. LXIX, No.95, 1971. Also Cammann, S.v.R., 'Symbolic Meanings in Oriental Rug Patterns', *Textile Museum Journal*, vol. III, No.3, 1972.
14. Thompson, J., *Von Konya bis Kokand*, Eberhart Herrmann III, München 1980.

Further reading

The works listed are a fraction of the literature available and include the more useful and accessible titles only.

General
- Hubel, R. G., *The Book of Carpets*, London 1971.
- Dilley, A.U. (rev. ed. by Dimand, M.S.), *Oriental Rugs and Carpets*, Lippincott, New York 1959.
- Denny, W., *Oriental Rugs*, Cooper Hewitt Museum, 1979.
- Spuhler, F., König H., Volkmann, M., *Old Eastern Carpets, Masterpieces in German Private Collections*, Callwey, München 1978.
- Dimand, M., Mailey, J., *Oriental Rugs in the Metropolitan Museum of Art*, New York 1973.

Specific topics
- Bidder, H., *Carpets from Eastern Turkestan*, Zwemmer, New York and London 1964.
- Bode W. v., Kühnel E., *Antique Rugs from the Near East* (tr. Ellis), Klinkhardt and Biermann, Braunschweig 1955.
- Denwood, P., *The Tibetan Carpet*, Aris and Phillips, Warminster 1974.
- Edwards, C., *The Persian Carpet*, Duckworth, London 1953.
- Ettinghausen, R. et al. *Prayer Rugs*, Textile Museum, Washington 1974.
- Housego, J., *Tribal Rugs, An Introduction to the Weaving of the Tribes of Iran*, Scorpion Publications, London 1978.
- Konieczny, M. G., *Textiles of Baluchistan*, British Museum 1979.
- Mackie, L., Thompson J., *Turkmen*, Textile Museum, Washington 1980.
- Mills, J., *Carpets in Pictures*, National Gallery, London 1975.
- Schürmann, U., *Caucasian Rugs*, Allen and Unwin, London 1976.
- Tschebull, R., *Kazak*, Near Eastern Research Centre and New York Rug Society, 1971.

Sources of illustrations

Acknowledgements

This book is the result of the collaboration of many parties and the author wishes to express his gratitude to those who have given support and kindly allowed their carpets and photographs to be used:

Wholesale traders
- L. Kelaty Ltd, Poole Street, London.
- P. & O. Carpets Ltd, Aldford Street, London.
- OCM (London) Ltd, who have asked me to state that they are suppliers exclusively to the trade.
  At the International Oriental Carpet Centre (IOCC), Highgate Road, London:
- Nathan and Joseph Azizolahoff,
- Yussef and Benyamin Bolour,
- Joseph Lavian,
- Nick Oundjian and London Oriental Carpets Ltd.

Retailers and galleries
- Apadana Carpets Ltd, Firouzan and Nematollahi, Ennismore Gardens, London.
- J. L. Arditti, Christchurch, Dorset.
- Atlantic Bay Carpets, Fulham Road, London.
- Avakian Oriental Carpets Ltd, Davies Street, London.
- Arky and Ginger Robbins, Baktiari Oriental Carpet Gallery, San Francisco.
- David Black Oriental Carpets, Portland Road, London.
- Simon Boosey, Whitwell, Hitchin, Herts.
- Cyrus Carpets, Piccadilly, London.
- Dinolevi, Florence.
- Eskenazi, Milan.
- Fairman Carpets, Westbourne Grove, London.
- Robert Franses, Nugent Terrace, London.
- Heskia, Mount Street, London.
- Alexander Juran and Co., Bond Street, London.
- Khalili Gallery, Clifford Street, London.
- D. W. Kinebanian, Amsterdam.
- Fritz Langauer of Adil Besim OHG, Vienna.
- Moutafian and Co. Ltd, Hammersmith Road, London.
- Paul Nels, South Molton Street, London.
- Clive Rogers, Oriental Carpets, Brighton, Sussex.
- The Rug Shop, Elystan Street, London.
- Shaikh and Son, Brook Street, London.
- Thornborough Galleries, Cirencester, Gloucestershire.
- A. Zadah, Persian Carpets, Dering Street, London.
  also:
- Richard Lannowe Hall of Lannowe Oriental Textiles, Marshfield, Wilts., specialists in conservation and cleaning, for his help and support.
- Jean Lefevre of Lefevre and Partners, Specialist Auctioneers, for the loan of photographs.
- The Mathaf Gallery, specialists in paintings of Middle Eastern interest, for the loan of the photograph of the watercolour by Charles Robertson.

Private collectors and collections
Mrs H. Andrews, Robert Attenborough, Mr and Mrs Paul Beck, Eric Bradley collection, A. S. Crosby, Lord Dufferin, Dr J. C. Hardy, Keir collection, Jane Oundjian, Wher collection, Neil Winterbottom, Marshall Wolf, Georgie Wolton, Richard Wright and all those who have not been named.

There are many others who have helped in innumerable different ways and I would like in particular to thank Michael Franses, David Black and Clive Loveless for the hours of work they have put in on my behalf; Christopher Weston and John Fisher for their efforts on the financial side; Malcolm Ward, copy editor, for his meticulous, attentive work and many helpful suggestions for the improvement of the text; J. P. J. Homer for his support; Jenny Housego, Josephine Powell, May Beattie, Jo Darrah, André Singer, Jorg Pfeiffer and Roy Macey for their generosity in lending valuable original photographic material; and to Roland Michaud, Eileen Graham, John Mills, Alistair Duncan, Jennifer Scarce, Eberhart Herrmann, Joss Graham, Peter Johnson and David Khalili, who have all put themselves out on my behalf; Peter John Gates for working to a tight time schedule in the photography of the carpets; and John Hoole, Curator of the Barbican Art Gallery, for his unfailing courtesy and patience.

Measurements
Irrespective of the shape or design, the length in the warp direction is given first.

Names and places
Iranians may be upset to find that their country is called Persia, except where a specific political entity is referred to. I hope they will understand that no disrespect to them or their country is intended. Persia is used because this is the name familiar to the English speaker through centuries of usage. Habits change slowly and it is used in the same way as one might use Munich for München or Ceylon for Sri Lanka.

Spellings of names generally agree with the rules of the Permanent Committee on Geographical Names. The main departures are where the rules demand a character not present on my typewriter. I have tended to leave the Turkish C when a rare name only likely to be found written in this form is used. But names familiar in western literature, for example Mujur, I have retained, because the more correct Mucur seems pedantic and confusing. Where the 'correct' spelling makes a well known name look unfamiliar I have desisted from using it.

The conflicting claims of transliteration systems compatible with Arabic, Roman and Cyrillic characters, and the different rules of spelling generated by the logic of Arabic, Turkish, Persian and the Turkic dialects can cause passions to rise to the point of apoplexy. I decided to avoid this problem by putting all the diacritical marks in a special form which renders them visible only to the initiated.

OVERLEAF: *This comfortable looking bag has a traditional design in the local style. Madder and indigo are still used to dye the wool. Shavak village, Tunceli province, Turkey.*